THE DISCERNING
GUIDE TO TRAVEL IN
FRACTIOUS AMERI

People to Visit and Places to Bombard

The 1770s Edition

Appendices hold student-friendly timeline,
to limit unnecessary exposure to grape shot

Contains added War of 1812 bicentenary flavouring

By

Dr Lee Rotherham

With an angry foreword by

Charles James Fox

Also by the same author

A Fate Worse Than Debt
The Discerning Barbarian's Guidebook to Roman Britain: People to Meet and Places to Plunder
The Sassenach's Escape Manual
The Discerning Mercenary's Guide to the Hundred Years War (coming in 2015)
The Tourist's Guide to Armageddon (coming whenever it gets written, ideally before the Apocalypse)

Foreword

by Charles James Fox

The war therefore was begun for the purpofe of alleviating the burthens of this country. Gentlemen, are you eafed, are you lightened? Have you felt the benefit of the American war in the decreafe of taxes, in the extenfion of your commerce, in the thriving ftate of opulence of your city? No. Your burthens have been doubled, and his Majefty's ministers have broken their Promifes with you. They have not drawn a revenue from America to alleviate the weight of your taxes, but inftead of this they have fpent more in difmembering the empire, that the great and good conductors of the laft war did in procuring the addition of Canada, and of all the advantages and glory which were gained to Great Britain at that time.

Westminster Hall speech, 10 December 1781

www.BretwaldaBooks.com
@Bretwaldabooks
bretwaldabooks.blogspot.co.uk/
Bretwalda Books on Facebook
First Published 2014

Bretwalda Books
Unit 8, Fir Tree Close, Epsom, Surrey KT17 3LD
info@BretwaldaBooks.com
www.BretwaldaBooks.com

ISBN 978-1-909698-80-2

Contents

An Introduction for Tourists

North America in the Later Colonial Period

The eighteenth century is a wonderful time for visiting the continent of North America, particularly if you are an Englishman. Travel in the seventeenth century can at times be brutish and, with the assistance of a tomahawk, occasionally short. Undertake travel later in the nineteenth century and one is required to focus much more on the occasionally brash but intriguingly vibrant young republic that is dominating centre stage.

However, by electing the middle period, as a traveller you are selecting a golden age. It is an époque where British influence reaches its zenith in these far-flung lands. An Englishman is able to travel without hindrance, without a passport, and even without leaving His Majesty's domains from the icy northern bays to the balmy Gulf. It is a time when the locals of the colonies, when announcing their intent to travel across the Atlantic to a land they have never seen, declare that they are "going home".

It's also a time when settlements are becoming more self-supporting, with increasingly impressive centres of learning in the professions as well as in the arts. The century is a period of genius, generating some of the greatest minds to step forth from the British people.

It's a time of exploration, of frontiers and adventure; of heroism, and drama; of cultures and contacts; of trade and riches, and indeed of controversial taxes too. You can explore for yourself the truth behind all those European myths, such as whether the environment is itself inherently ruinous for creating any meaningful society (a falsehood) or is so conducive to good health that the locals are a good two inches taller than those brought up in the stink holes of London (which is correct).

An awareness of progression helps. That's why we include at the end in the appendices a handy timeline for students, to help you avoid getting shot as a spy.

So this handbook is a guidebook to help the gentleman as he goes about his mission in the country. It's part survival guide, part tome to assist in cultural acclimatisation, part aide-memoire to help manage expectations in what remains a frontier land. With careful planning, common sense (not Common Sense: see later) and the occasional prod, there's no reason why the visitor can't have an invigorating trip or undertake a successful business venture without losing his scalp or ending up on a prison hulk.

Chapter 1

Planning Your Visit

Tourist Seasons

For ease of reference, we divide the visiting times up into seasons, since the conditions will vary for travellers considerably over time.

Those travelling Out of Season (up to 1700) should reference our sister guidebook, Burying the Hatchet: How to Survive Your First Winter in the New World. This provides a much fuller background to handling this rough-and-ready pioneer setting. Nevertheless, this period of course establishes the context for much of what follows and so we have included into our summary timeline a review of the key aspects that will be of interest.

The High Season runs from 1700 to 1763, which is when everyone will want to come here. The future great cities of the coast are beginning to take shape, and are starting to compete with the provincial towns of England in being able to provide for the needs of a comfortable and pleasant life. The ambitious meanwhile can still cut a name for themselves on the frontiers. Since the continent is hotly contested by three great European powers, there is a strong cultural vibrancy at play and the well-travelled man can contrast the differing colonial empires. They may not be London, Madrid or Paris, but these outposts provide tasters of the different societies implanting their footprint across the Atlantic.

Mid Season runs from 1763 to 1783. It begins with the high water mark of the British Empire, as all North America of any consequence is united in British hands through the Treaty of Paris. But a number of factors then conspire to bring utter ruin to the enterprise. The removal of the French threat means there is no unifying existential danger for the colonies. The British have to keep troops garrisoned in the area to keep the Indian frontier secured, which costs money, and which the locals don't want to pay. To keep those costs down, the Crown has to reach an agreement with the Indians which means stopping the colonists from encroaching on their lands and starting wars, which the colonists also don't like. It's a no-win scenario that the colonials simply don't grasp. Back in Britain, the country is so massively in debt from fighting all these wars that the taxpayers are taxed to the hilt; yet try and get the colonial merchants to stop smuggling and habitually trading with the enemy, and to cough up a few pence worth of taxes themselves, and you get accused of despotism. Ultimately the whole potage goes badly wrong. As this season goes on, the book will be of particular use to those seeking to avoid faux pas in dinner conversations (particularly around hysterical Boston), and as a billeting guide to those gentlemen who are serving with their regiments against the rebels. Pay particular attention to survival sections in the Carolinas where the niceties of warfare amongst gentlemen are increasingly being forgotten.

Low Season covers 1783 to 1815. Tragically, opportunities have been missed to settle the constitutional differences, and (though this is no given) the rebels win the American War of Independence. This again splinters British North America, with France and Spain briefly regaining their footholds. Travellers now will be able to explore the mushrooming republic, but also quietly marvel at how the remaining colonies to its north have managed to move on from the harrowing times and themselves eke out a footing in the wilderness. Your stay may also coincide with the War of 1812, a confused and far-ranging conflict that becomes steadily less respectful of property. It is a time of heroism as the Canadians themselves play a key role in repelling several serious attacks on their lands, and their successes will play a major part in establishing a sense of identity in this other emerging American nation.

Whichever season you choose to travel in, you can be assured of a warm (and occasionally, toasty) welcome, and the adventure of an (occasionally brief) lifetime.

Highlights

1 French North America

Whether you choose to visit while still under rule from Paris, or care to stay while under British control, a trip to Quebec and Montreal proves thought-provoking for how history might have turned out very differently for this continent.

2 Indians

The indigenous peoples of America live very differently. Take a culturally rewarding trip, barter for precious furs, or stay awhile and learn vital survival skills.

3 Colonial cities

Boston, New York, Philadelphia and Charleston are the colonial hubs, with Halifax as an increasingly key harbour. Explore these vibrant ports whose strong imperial links make them closer to London than to one another.

4 The tragedy of the Acadiens

Acadie is a frontiersman's place and far from the blissful Acadia of Greek myth. But its people make their own legend.

5 Tea in Boston

Forget the 'Boston Tea Party', a night time spot of fancy dress vandalism. Instead, make the most of the opportunities on offer to indulge in some bargain basement sales and take tea on the waterfront.

6 Beyond the frontier

Make a fortune in trapping or a name for yourself exploring. Perhaps you won't find El Dorado, but you can name a river after yourself instead.

7 Pick a Pirate

No need to go all the way down to the Caribbean to meet these fascinating scoundrels. Hang around Newfoundland or New York in the early eighteenth century, or even better visit the Carolinas to catch sight of the infamous Edward Teach himself.

8 Wolfe's Triumph

A bold strike, an astonishing victory, the death of a hero, the conquest of a nation. Watch the victory unfold.

9 Meet George Washington

From defeated colonial commander to a victorious general and the country's first President, chat with the man who endured the bitter winter of Valley Forge, and who turned down a crown.

10 Building a Nation

How do you decide a constitution? Witness the debates first hand as the statesmen grapple with a revolutionary form of government, and rights and liberties are battled out.

Getting there

> "The mouth of the River of St Lawrence, and more especially the Bay of St Lawrence, lyes so far North, and is thereby so often subject to the tempestuous weather and thick Fogs, that the navigation there is very dangerous, and never attempted, but during the summer months. The wideness of the Bay, together with ye many strong currents that run in it, the many shelves and sunken rocks that are every where spread over both the Bay and River, and the want of places for anchoring in the Bay, all increase the dangers of this navigation. So that a voyage to Canada is justly esteemed much more dangerous than to any other part of America."
>
> Extract of a report from Cadwallader Colden, His Majesty's Surveyor in New York, 10 November 1724

Shipping

There are a number of possible access routes to North America. The key trading port on our side of the ocean is London, not least as it is such a large population centre and as a result has a huge local market that draws the shipping. The Thames is tidal and this provides merchants with easy access up the estuary even with a contrary wind, an advantage shared by only two other river cities in Europe. But it does mean though that on leaving the city you may have to wait further down the coast for the wind to change – a final opportunity for some homely meat pies before you sail.

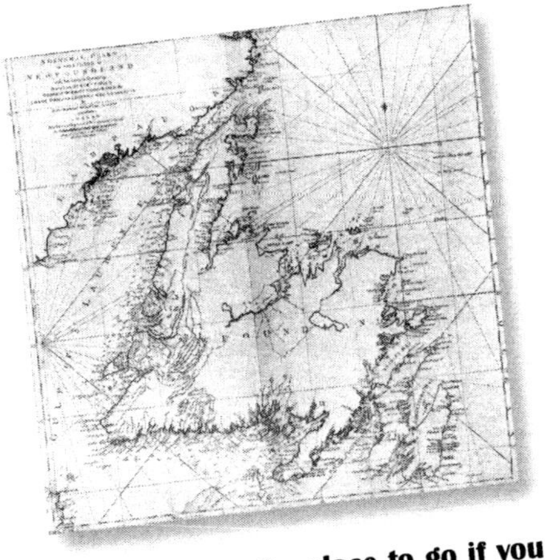

Newfoundland is the place to go if you are in the fish business as the waters are famously full of cod. For everyone else it is a bit chilly and off the beaten track.

Swiftly growing in importance is Liverpool. It's only a small village at the turn of the eighteenth century, but the establishment of docks, and in the latter part of the century city control over dock financing, have guaranteed its expansion. It becomes a key port involved in the triangular slave trade; merchandise goes to Africa, to buy slaves which are shipped to the colonies, there to buy local products such as cotton for the Lancashire mills.

That will be too indirect a route for yourself. Consider as alternatives the port of Bristol, particularly if heading for the north east since it has exceptional ties with Newfoundland. Whitehaven and Scarborough in the north of England are both very important ports, and as such will attract American privateers during the rebellion. Minehead is an alternative in the south west, and Glasgow in Scotland. So you shouldn't be lacking an embarkation point if sailing from Britain. Note though that if setting off from outside the British Isles, trading laws may well prevent your foreign ship from sailing direct so you may need to change ship at one of the harbours above.

The quality of your trip will vary. Clearly, if you can afford to pay for a cabin you'll find the privacy and airiness of your accommodation a far less oppressive regime than stuck below decks. You might also find a southerly route longer but less squally, though this of course rather depends on when you are sailing as there is a defined safe season. We would also recommend bringing additional provision with you to ensure you have your customary luxuries. Expect a voyage to last anywhere between one month or two, depending on winds.

In the southern colonies in particular, a large portion of your local travelling may well be by boat given the number of rivers bisecting the landscape. Travelling between colonial cities more generally may often be best achieved by coastal vessels. Ask for a sloop heading to your destination. You might find barges plying the waters to the north though these are not built for accommodation so be prepared to rough it.

There are around 40 official ports of entry, so your choice of destination is as varied as the land you are visiting itself.

Roads

The eighteenth century is seeing some major advances with the colonial road network. In part this can be attributed to frontiersmen pushing the boundaries of civilisation into the hinterland and beyond what is most immediately accessible from the river systems, which remain the most obvious routes for shipping trade goods. The postal service also spurs investment in improving ancient Indian paths, bare bridleways and foot-pressed tracks, with ferries providing important links in the chain. Note that you will have to pay a charge if travelling on your own account and if not on public business, though the fee should be set by law.

By the middle of the century something approaching a colonial great road has been built which in parts is of superior quality. However, a number of the roads are still very wearisome, badly maintained, and the coach driver may require your assistance in removing clutter from the track. Connecticut's routes have a particularly bad reputation. Carolina's are subject to another peril - bad relations with the local Indians. Note that roads are particularly treacherous during periods of bad weather, and potentially impassable especially in the north during winter.

The first 'national' (or federal road) starts to get built in the early nineteenth century, pushing into the Ohio area and heading generally out west. Who knows where the western end will one day end up.

Portage

One rather exciting opportunity that may present itself is if you intend to travel well off the beaten track. Travelling the hinterland can take the explorer far across rugged and unfamiliar landscapes. Waterways provide ready access, but to exploit them successfully the best technique is to follow Indian practice. The canoe is a lightweight, portable vehicle for paddling up slow moving rivers, and descending the faster ones, but adaptable enough to be picked up and manhandled across the difficult bits. That's despite the size some of these beasts can get to. Navigating them is an acquired skill, as is spotting the signs for getting off the river to safely nip by a danger point on foot, so we would recommend hiring a team of experts or linking up with a group intending to head inland on a fur expedition.

A cart for carrying canoes from one river to another.
Better than carrying them.

The most celebrated of such groups are the voyageurs. These are rugged French Canadian outdoorsmen, the long-range successors to the coureurs de bois. Stereotypically, they wear a floppy hat that drapes down one side of their face called a tuque; and perhaps a ceinture flêchée or colourful woven woollen belt, one of whose ends they knot. The image is complete if they have a shaggy beard and a prim little pipe too – you might even find them using the latter as a measurement of time. Up a creek without a paddle? Not with this lot.

If you've come to North America for adventure, and if you can endure the lifestyle and the really hard work, you might find a canoe voyage is right up your street (or river). Remember though it's certainly no place for slackers.

Safe Passage

Gentlemen not in uniform should note that travel during times of conflict runs the tedious risk of your falling in with privateers. While a number of these are men of quality, some are little more than pirates, and some are indeed actual pirates. The best rule is to follow the instructions of your vessel's captain. As a rule of thumb, if the enemy has more cannon than you, and is behind your stern just about to rake the length of your ship, you'll probably want to surrender.

If you do become a prisoner, try to avoid giving your parole, or bond not to try to escape, as there may be opportunities to attempt it. This is particularly the case if there are doughty navy or army types who are fellow prisoners. We suggest you go with the flow, always remembering that if you have given your word, as a gentleman you should stick by it.

Privateers are a real threat. In the War of Independence, the American Navy captures or destroys just under 200 vessels, but the privateers achieve three times that figure. In the War of 1812, their regular navy is not much bigger and captures around 250, but the privateers take about 1300 ships. With just about anybody owning a keel putting a Yankee cannon on it, there are over five hundred ships ranging about the waves trying to find unsuspecting easy pickings. The Royal Navy can't be everywhere at once. So do take care. It will even cause a scare in linen ships travelling just between Ireland and England in the 1770s, a panic that the great fleets of France and Spain never generated.

Weather

Obviously, North America is a continent, covering many degrees of latitude. You should pack according to the zone you will be staying in. Tropical storms are a risk particularly in the south, which is also hotter. The north is more temperate and reminiscent of home, though even Virginia can catch you unawares if you are not used to humidity.

August and September are the peak period for storms, which are more of a problem the further south you go nearer the Tropics. They can be a major risk for shipping. None have matched the Great Hurricane of 1635 (which happily skirted the English colonies but did sink a ship), but do be sure to leave the United States before September 1815 to dodge the Great Gale, as this will cause significant damage and interrupt your transport timetable.

Seasons

The seasons match those in England, but are more intense in their application. Travellers should consider this when packing clothing before departure, as they may have to endure a few days at sea subject to the rigours of the latitude before being able to purchase replacement costume.

In particular, northern winters around New France are especially arduous, and can get so cold that a man's breathe freezes instantly in his nose on opening the door. Bitter winds can reduce the temperature even more. If one uses the scale lately proffered by Mr Fahrenheit, we suggest a bad day might be as low as minus 22, and taking wind into account minus 58. In these conditions, wear clothing to survive, not to impress on account of misplaced London style.

Surprisingly, you will find New England a cooler wintry clime than cities of equal latitude back in Europe, so factor this into your packing. It need hardly be said that as the continent drops to the area of the Caribbean colonies, summer's heat will be exaggerated.

Easing your Journey

Travel takes time. Ease it with an investment that will make your arrival particularly popular, by splashing out on a first edition of a popular book that you can lend or gift to associates in the colonies;

1719 - Robinson Crusoe (Daniel Defoe): a shipwreck (perhaps not best reading).

1722 - Moll Flanders (Daniel Defoe): a sordid life story with an American connection.

1726 - Gulliver's Travels (Jonathan Swift): more shipwrecks.

1748 - Clarissa (Samuel Richardson): an evocative tragedy.

1749 - The History of Tom Jones, A Foundling (Henry Fielding): social betterment in the context of vice. Many volumes so make sure you have plenty of packing space.

1755 – A Dictionary of the English Language (Samuel Johnson): useful for arguing over colonial spelling.

1759+ The Life and Opinions of Tristram Shandy, Gentleman (Laurence Sterne): several volumes, of entertainingly rambling divergence.

1773 - She Stoops to Conquer (Oliver Goldsmith): play about mistaken identity and assumed class.

1775 - The Rivals (Richard Sheridan): play, which coins the term Malapropism from a character.

1776 - The Wealth of Nations (Adam Smith): economics for beginners, ie everybody.

1776+ The Decline and Fall of the Roman Empire (Edward Gibbon): a well-crafted history of Rome, published over many years so bring the latest volume.

1789 - Equiano's Travels: The Interesting Narrative of the Life of Olaudah Equiano or Gustavus Vassa the African (Olaudah Equiano): anti-slavery autobiography.

1790 - The Marriage of Heaven and Hell (William Blake): biblical script and striking artwork. Make sure you get your lent copy back.

1798 – Lyrical Ballads. Contains The Rime of the Ancient Mariner (Samuel Taylor Coleridge): tips on what not to do with an albatross. Also contains work by William Wordsworth.

Geography

Britain's Thirteen Colonies are bounded by nature itself. Their eastern limits are fringed by the Atlantic Ocean. To the west, civilisation and settlement is reaching sufficiently to the interior to consider the Appalachian mountain chain as its boundary. Beyond that is territory the French have declared as their own, a claim contended by the British who have formed their own agreements with certain Indian tribes who also claim sway over parts of the vast interior.

The colonies themselves can be divided into three blocks. New England to the north is rocky, with poor quality soils (excepting parts of Massachusetts) and plenty of trees. This makes them more reliant on the sea. The Mid colonies have better soil and a better climate for agriculture. The South is even better, with long growing seasons, mild winters, and great tidal rivers allowing for good access, but also making some areas swampy. Wildlife provides excellent hunting and trapping opportunities.

The northern and southern frontiers are problematic. New England's border with New France has largely been a matter of respectful distance, with untamed woods providing a buffer zone. With increased population those distances have, however, shrunk. New France's urban hinterland is focused on the great Saint Lawrence river. That civilisation's lower reaches was spread over the territory known as Acadie, largely and later completely conquered and turned into Nova Scotia. This stretch of woods and coast is if you like the rugged northern shoulder of the old English colonies. Arching out into the Atlantic is the huge island of Newfoundland, barren marshy and mist-soaked rock but bounded by astonishing teeming fisheries.

In the south the English colonies are from 1670 separated by a line on paper, but in reality are determined by the population of settlements and it is the British who are doing most of the settling. The exact frontier is politically controversial and seemingly always on the move.

Almost beyond the touch of civilisation there is also the area to the far north. The Labrador coast is bleak and desolate, unless you happen to be a Moravian missionary or a fur trader. Fur is also responsible for the series of outposts dotted around the interior coastline of the vast Hudson (or Hudson's) Bay. James Bay is the huge inlet that cuts south of the main stretch. Prince Rupert's Land is the vast trading empire that is the territory that lies around the whole bay, but also extending south west into the continental hinterland.

The Peoples

A Micmac family outside their home.

There is no uniformity in His Majesty's colonies. Indeed, that is both a part of their tourist appeal, and a reason why colonists seem at times to get on with one another so badly!

Take the case of Pennsylvania. It was founded largely by the Quakers, though increasingly a number of Anglican settlers made up a share of the population, concentrated in the farmland in the south east. From the 1720s onwards there are a large number of German settlers (by the Revolution they make up a third of the population). These move in to farm the interior. Besides these, the Ulster Scots and Scots come over at around the same time and move into the western valleys and engage on major frontiers clearing, and they make up a quarter of the population by the 1770s. There are also Dutch and Swedes appearing, a Welsh community in the east, and a notable Jewish community.

Contrast that for example with Boston. Massachusetts was overwhelmingly at one point a Puritan colony, but they weren't the original religious colonists. That honour went to the Pilgrim settlers. The arrival of the Puritans may have been something of a culture shock to the founders, who wanted to escape from the established church rather than reform it. So much for making a clean break. In any event, religious revivalism re-emerges in the

1730s, turning the colony into a hotbed of religious competition and one-upmanship. It also increasingly attracts a reputation as politically volatile.

For reference you'll often hear talk of New England. What is it? Just think of everywhere north east of New York. New England is made up of Connecticut, New Hampshire, Massachusetts (including the stretch later known as Maine), Rhode Island and Vermont.

How very different are the societies of Maryland and Virginia. Planters there run the lives of local aristocrats, occupying great houses, with estates maintained by slaves; while in smaller plots free farmers labour to make a living. But with no need for middlemen there is no great shipping and trading class.

Listen carefully and you might notice distinct accent traits. Some gentlemen who have made a study of such matters suggest that there are four main regional accents. Massachusetts betrays the East Anglian accent; southern American betrays upper class exiled cavaliers; Delaware, Quakers from the northern Midlands; Scots-Irish mannerisms meanwhile underpin the accent of the Appalachians. Add to this the foreign influence: Brooklyn shows a hint of underlying Dutch.

Perhaps though the greatest cultural difference is between those living in the civilised coastal areas and those on the edge. Having cut away the woodland, these pioneers (such people as the French call "défricheurs") live a make-do existence. They go hunting in practical deerskin. They dine on what they can catch and hunt. They have loud parties where they burn food to a cinder and shoot things. They also have horizons that stretch westwards and not across the ocean, unless they have brought those old ties with them as first generation immigrants.

The Canadians of Québec

Canada is French territory. But it is a magical New World France. Even when the French are still here, the society has grown distinct from the homeland. Once the colonial governors have gone, leaving their colonists, the distinct imprint endures. It is overwhelmingly Roman Catholic, first by nationality and by French royal law, and secondly after the Conquest as a

Whitehall concession to secure their loyalty. It is also a society that becomes largely folded in on itself as a defence mechanism against an overwhelmingly British continent. To preserve their exposed community, priests encourage large families, large even by American standards; a good wife should aim to "faire sa douzaine" - produce a dozen children - in order to provide enough offspring to keep their society alive. Certainly, any trip to its main metropoles may surprise you with the number and visibility of priests and nuns, considering the lack of freedom granted by Parliament to Catholics elsewhere, including back home.

The excesses of the French Revolution, particularly towards the Church, subsequently drive an irreversible wedge between Paris and its erstwhile colonies. The solidly church-going French Canadians learn to distrust revolution, and mistrust their traditional enemies to the south in the emerging United States.

Within a separate Canada, and as the Crown opens up government a chink, some of the landed gentry start to play a noted role in society as community leaders. In the Low Season, this includes participation and even key leadership posts in local militias.

French Canadians have long held a reputation as experienced wilderness survivalists, and expert hit-and-run irregulars. They respect their environment and prepare for it. You would be advised to acknowledge their abilities in the field, especially when they are deployed with Indian allies.

The accent may confuse you, used as you are to being taught Court French as enounced at Versailles. In fact, as you travel across the Province you'll find the accent jumps. Out east in Nova Scotia and old Acadie, the Acadiens (and after them the Cajuns) are largely the descendants of the Poitevins and emigrants from Saintonge. Technically, this makes them the descendants of the lost English Empire of Aquitaine. Many of the Québécois for their part are of Norman extraction, making them the descendants of the lost English Empire of Henry V. Perhaps history in a strange way is compensating for England losing the Hundred Years War! But as you travel widely across the various are, you'll find - even more markedly than in the British colonies - local differences in dialects that mirror what the accents from the home provinces in France were when they set out a century or more ago.

So the politics changes but society endures. To help you with the former, we'll keep the accents in the names when discussing places while they are still under French rule.

Acadiens

The destiny of the French colonists of Acadie, which later becomes Nova Scotia, New Brunswick and Prince Edward Island, is a poignant one. Most of their territory was conquered a good three decades before Quebec. That left them in British hands. But very quickly, local priests were stirring up Indians against the new colonial power, supported by the French colonial administration. Worse, it generated real problems and actual fighting not once but twice after the handover. As war with France loomed again, the limited pledge offered by local residents of Acadien neutrality was not considered to be enough, and a British governor resolved to deport them so they couldn't back the French in wartime. With 13,000 of them in the area, any commander reviewing the isolated British settlements could see their presence could prove key.

It begins with a ban on the use of guns and canoes. Then, in 1755 the plans are announced. The intention was to keep families together, but so keen is the governor to remove the men they are prioritised. Meanwhile, homes are destroyed and livestock confiscated to ensure that no one hides.

A number do hide, living out in the woods, or making their way gradually to French territory. Some founded new settlements that are raided in turn by British forces seeking to evict them. They will live this precarious existence until the Seven Years War is over, and the territorial threat France played finally settled. With no further prospect of French invasion, the local residents can no longer act as a fifth column, have no reason to rouse the Micmac tribes to attack the British settlements, and so are no longer a threat. A number of Acadiens who agree to take the oath of allegiance trickle back. Those who had resettled in Louisbourg and the coastal fringes, however, are considered irredeemably French and expelled.

Acadien culture is perhaps a fairly rough one. Their main town is Port Royal, which is hardly a preeminent urban setting.

Their communities are largely rural, farming ones. Large families mean strong community relations as neighbours marry over the years. The Catholic priest is a central figure in the community; indeed, one of the major symbols of the disruption caused to society by the deportation is the image of the makeshift mass taking place without the priest.

A number of the expelled choose to stay behind in their places of exile. The Cajuns of Louisiana in particular keep an echo of their former name, and have swapped the snows of the north for the water life of the bayou.

Perhaps water is in their soul. In Acadie, they were known for the way a number of their settlements had cleverly reclaimed marshland. The aboiteau in particular is an ingenious sluice that opens at low tide, but which the rising high tide closes off again. The dyke system is a key feature of the landscape and the secret to reclaiming what becomes fine agricultural land. It's also something that requires a community spirit to keep operational.

When visiting, if you're from a farming background in Norfolk or Lincolnshire, you might appreciate their use of what the sea has to offer. For example, they exploit salt marsh grasses from the tidal area as winter fodder, storing it on platforms above high water mark.

All told, you won't go hungry visiting a settled Acadian village. There's plenty of livestock meats, vegetables, wild fowl and woods fare to vary your dish. Get used to barley bread in some parts. Dip into the pies. Most definitely, do test out the beer, which is part based on fir tree shoots, or risk a sniff of the dandelion wine.

Do note though that educational standards are not high, so expect low literacy: you may need the assistance of the priest to get anything signed. By contrast, there's a strong oral tradition to make up for it, with plenty a song about the rugged seas or distant gloomy lonely woods.

So for a romantic holiday, pick Acadie in the summer. Just don't leave it til the second half of the century, or it may be as part of utopian history as the Arcadia in ancient Greece it was named after.

The Métis

Not all French Canadians plump for a life of cutting back the wilderness and building communities. For some, the allure of the wilds and the wealth that furs can bring are reasons enough to live life on the edge. We encountered these voyageurs earlier, the traders whose vast trading routes provide France with an imprint across the hinterland of the continent and a (tenuous) claim on these lands.

Living amongst the natives has a further consequence though. Many assimilate into the communities with which they spend so much time, including by marriage. This creates generations of descendants who are part French, part Indian. Particularly with the conquest, the expansion of the traders from the Hudson Bay increases Anglo-Indian marriages, in which we include a significant number of Scots who contribute so much to exploring these wildernesses, and whose wives sometimes accompany them as guides, interpreters, and camp sharers.

Some Métis might follow in their father's footsteps and bring their skills and language abilities to the fur company. Others might follow the traditions rather of the tribe.

Their existence becomes more widely known with the moves to settle the mid plains around the Red River Valley, triggering a conflict that we suspect will store up major problems ahead.

The Métis of the prairies are masters of the bison hunt. This is hardly surprising, given the astonishing variety of uses the beast can be put to. Its skin can be used to make clothing, footwear and fabrics; its horns are used for arrows and utensils; its bones are useful for making tools; its fat serves as soap or fuel; and of course there's the meat too. On the Great Plains where trees can be scarce, the bison can be a true walking resource.

Not everyone is a ready master of new languages. Striking up an association with a member of this community could be an easier way to get an insight into native life away from the easy supports of trades and civilisation.

The Colonies

As you are travelling around North America, you may find it useful to consider how it was that a particular area came to be established and then attracted settlers. It may go some way to explaining the locals. So here's a little list to help get you started.

Colony Name	*Year Founded*	*Founded By*	*Motivation*
Virginia	1607 (first enduring settlement)	London Company	Business venture.
New Jersey	1618 (first occupied)	Dutch trading post	Proper settlement and establishment took place in the 1660s and initially driven by Quakers seeking freedom of religion.
Massachusetts	1620 (first successful settlement)	Puritans	Freedom to practise religion (radical protestants).
New Hampshire	1623 (first settlement)	John Mason, David Thompson	Fishing colony opportunity for settlers.
New York (founded as New Amsterdam; renamed 1664)	1624 (first settlement)	Dutch West India Company	Bolster existing trading post.
Maryland	1634 (first settlement)	Cecil Calvert a.k.a. Lord Baltimore	Freedom to practise religion (Roman Catholics).
Connecticut	1635 (first settlement)	Thomas Hooker	Expansion from Massachusetts.
Providence Plantation (Rhode Island)	1636 (first settlement)	Roger Williams	Dissidents banished from Massachusetts over allowing freedom of conscience.

Delaware	1638 (first successful settlement)	New Sweden Company	Swedish colonial experiment seized by Dutch. Captured by Britain 1664. Separate legislature 1702.
North Carolina	1653 (first successful settlement)	Virginians	Expansion.
South Carolina	1663 (first settlement)	Group of nobles	Financial investment. Carolinas divided in 1729.
Pennsylvania	1682 (first settlement)	William Penn	Territory received in lieu of repayment of royal debt, as a place to practise freedom of religion (Quakers).
Georgia	1733 (first settlement)	James Oglethorpe	Prison reform: colony for former inmates. Bulwark against Spanish imperial frontier.
'Non-Thirteen' Colonies			
Florida	1565 (first successful settlement)	Don Pedro Menéndez de Avilés	Protection of southern trade routes.
Acadie/New Brunswick	1604 (first unsuccessful settlement, technically now in Maine)	Samuel de Champlain	French fur trade. Survivors founded Nova Scotia. NB separated off from Nova Scotia after Loyalist settlement in 1784.
Acadie/Nova Scotia	1605 (first successful settlement)	Samuel de Champlain	French fur trade.
Quebec (Lower Canada, 1791)	1608 (first settlement)	Samuel de Champlain	Improved site upriver for competitive French access to fur trade.

Newfoundland	1610 (first settlement)	John Guy	Control and protection of major cod fisheries.
Upper Canada (1791)	1668 (mission established at existing settlement)	Jacques Marquette	French mission of Sault Ste-Marie at a native village, which became a fur trade centre.
Prince Rupert's Land	1684 (lasting headquarters and "factory")	Hudson's Bay Company	Fur trade centre.
French Mississippi territories	1699 (first trading links established that would create a market)	Pierre Le Moyne d'Iberville	In 1720 Biloxi is briefly appointed colonial capital, before it is transferred to New Orleans.
St John's Island (from 1799, Prince Edward Island)	1720 (first permanent settlement)	Michel Haché-Gallant	Acadiens moving after Treaty of Utrecht; site supports/protects French fishing rights.
Ohio and the old 'North West'	1772 (first civilian settlement)	David Zeisberger	Freedom to practise religion (Moravians). Forced to withdraw owing to Revolution. First lasting settlement in 1788.

Strange Little Republics

In an age of ambitious revolutionaries, and continuing colonial outposts, we perhaps shouldn't be too surprised to find additional little republics popping up now and again, as local residents or adventurers scheme to carve themselves out a little New World niche, and others are driven by patriotism to bolt their lands onto the English-speaking world.

Take for instance the Republic of West Florida. West Florida is the stretch of the Spanish colony that adjoins the French territories of Louisiana. The exact border is a little shaky, and there are increasing numbers of Americans who have been settling the area. Thus in September 1810, hearing that the new governor is looking at arresting a number of them for daring to demand political reform, a group of conspirators make a pre-emptive blow and seize Baton Rouge. Up goes a new flag, a white star on blue background. Three months later, the US Government moves in.

Or consider the obscure Watauga Association. In the 1760s, the Regulator Movement had tried to change the way that South Carolina had been governed. That escalated badly and was crushed. Some settlers decide to up sticks and leave, heading off into what would later be known as Tennessee. Doing a deal with the Cherokee for land, from 1772-1775 they run their own affairs as an unofficial self-governing republic. From 1776 they form an association with North Carolina.

In 1784 though, North Carolina hands over its western territories to the federal government while the local residents campaign for statehood of their own. The residents of the Watauga Association now set up their own government, the State of Franklin. This lasts a year. North Carolina repeals its decision to hand over the land; the US Senate decides against recognising and admitting the new state, which isn't that big anyway; and the land is absorbed again by North Carolina.

To these we might add the peculiar status of Vermont. New Hampshire and New York in the 1750s and 1760s are involved in a serious dispute over where their borders lie, an argument that centred on land claims known as the New Hampshire Grants. The residents understandably are unhappy at New York's intention to declare the granting of land to them by New Hampshire illegal, and in effect they secede just before the Revolutionary War began. This creates a republic that neither neighbouring Loyalists nor Revolutionaries are particularly happy with. In 1781, some of their leaders are involved in negotiations to join the Loyalist cause in return for territorial concessions: these talks though are overtaken by events. In 1791, the United States agrees to accept the territory as a state and the powder keg issue is settled.

Indian Territory

Throughout this guide book we refer to the natives as Indians. This is traditional. If there is a better way of describing the original inhabitants from before the founding of the first settlements, we do not yet know it.

There are several determining features that distinguish between the various tribes. You might in your dealings with them consider the following;

* Does the tribe live largely in woods, or on the plains?
* Does the tribe live in areas that have exhausted its fur supply?
* Does the tribe have an obvious need for particular goods?
* Do they speak a common language?
* Is it a tribe that has long had dealings with the British?
* Have those dealings traditionally been - largely - friendly?
* Does the tribe, alternatively, traditionally form alliances with the French?
* Has that tribe been decisively defeated in a war?
* Have any colonists recently angered the tribe by stealing their land?

* How does the tribe relate to other tribes, and what fallout is happening from what is happening to them?

Given a moment's consideration, wandering up to a (pro-French) Huron encampment in the midst of a French war may not thus be the most prudent survival move.

Here are some words on the main tribes you might hear about, to get you started.

Tribes

As far as the tourist is concerned, the Indians might usefully be grouped into five categories. The first is the isolated type that he might be extremely unlikely to meet. The second are those who have historically sided with the French. The third are the ones that have largely sided with the British. The fourth are the ones whose names will be familiar from tales of old settlement, but whose significance has faded or been broken as the colonies have expanded to the point of no longer living a knife-edge existence dependent on keeping them happy. The final group are those whose power remains strong and whose position on the undeveloped edge of empire means that they are important players in continental politics.

Let's take a tour of the main tribes you might hear about. We'll start with one you'll have some real difficulties coming across. The local tribe to Newfoundland is a small group known as the Beothuk. They are part of the Algonquin group, though somewhat cut off. Initially the presence of European fishermen was useful, since they left behind all manner of scraps of tools and metals when they sailed home for the winter. Scavenging also meant that they didn't need to make contact with the Europeans, and adapt their ways to accommodate them through trade. But when permanent settlements arrive, it means that they are unable to adapt and keep themselves totally apart. As a result, while culturally they have kept to their old ways, you'll likely not get to see them. This may be a good thing for you, as with increasing clashes with trappers, the natives have come to fear the outsiders. An attempt in 1811 to establish peaceful official contacts ends in two men dead. From what little we know of this dwindling community we can only surmise that this is a people that is running out of time.

Over on the mainland are what might be styled the French tribes. The French colonies are significantly less populated than the British ones, meaning that they are both less a cause for tension with the native peoples, and also the colonists are more encouraged by manpower shortages to make use of the Indians as allies. But it also has brought the French in turn their own problems, as alliances mean allying against the enemies of your friend.

Prominent are the Algonquins, whose lands stretch across the upper lakes and down the river to the sea. It's important to distinguish here between the tribe of that name, and the tribal group. A number of tribes are broadly related and speak connected languages, and indeed a number of these in fact were originally settled in New England and which we'll come to in a bit. So when we hear talk about the Algonquins in general terms we may be encountering a blanket term that covers a lot of tribes and a lot of politics. But when we hear talk about the French allies called the Algonquins, we're discussing a French-allied society in the north.

These, like other French allies the Hurons, were devastatingly mauled by the Iroquois in the seventeenth century, who also destroyed the Jesuit missions the French had sent there. Both these tribes were forced to resettle nearer to French towns. They are famed for their canoes, enterprisingly fabricated from birch bark, making them lighter to handle than the more solid craft of other tribes. Socially they are fascinating, and share a number of aspects with their bitter enemies. They perhaps gave the Iroquois the original idea of forming a confederation of tribes. Women are important, with descent traced through them. They farm, though lack concepts of crop rotation and so move their settlements generationally - an event that triggers the Feast of the Dead. This unique Huron event involves digging up those who had died natural deaths, scraping clean their bones, and reburying them in a common grave in a massive ceremony so their spirits could finally depart to the west. Don't worry - the feasting part is separate.

The Micmacs meanwhile are a tribe in northern Acadie. They have persistently been a nuisance to His Majesty's interests, stirred up first through repeated troublemaking by the French and now latterly by the American revolutionaries. As long as Nova Scotia remains unsettled they will remain an important force in the area. The Abenakis reside further to the south and enjoy good links with them, including participating in sundry wars with English colonists.

By contrast, the Iroquois have lately proven to be our strongest allies. You may hear talk of them as the Five Nations, since this is the nature of the Iroquois Confederacy (at least until a sixth one joins in the 1720s). Although the Algonquin peoples had settled down the coast as far as Delaware, the interior as far as the Lakes is today Iroquois following a great period of conquests in the late 1600s when they crushed their opponents, forcing them to flee to the French. The interior has now seen a massive shift in power.

The cause of this was the struggle between the tribes to control the lucrative supply of pelts, whence the name of Beaver Wars.

It would be an error of the first magnitude to assume that their run-ins with the French have always made them our friends, or that these fierce warriors who have conquered much of the hinterland are subservient. Do not assume either that these people are walkovers. On several occasions disputes with British colonial authorities have come close to triggering war, so treat them with respect.

During the revolution, the Americans achieve what the French could never quite do: splitting the confederacy. The Tuscarora and the Oneida align with the revolutionaries, while the Mohawk, Seneca, Onondaga and Cayuga stay loyal to the Crown.

The Iroquois are culturally perhaps most famous because of their longhouses. Picture them as a cross between something from Beowulf, and a barn. Each may house a score of families communally with precious little privacy, other than that generated by the fact of sleeping on one of the side platforms. There are small holes to let smoke from the fires out, but inside is generally dark. The building is perhaps something of a metaphor for the group's political structures, bringing together different tribes under a shared political roof. Some say that their Great Law, defining differences in government between the executive, legislative and judicial, may end up giving the colonists some funny ideas of their own. It is certainly the case that individuals are given considerable freedom and responsibility in a form of democracy.

Of the old east coast tribes, you may hear talk of the Delawares, who are actually the Lenape living in the territories being settled by Lord De La Warr. The tribal family reaches up as far as Connecticut. Relations with the British have been increasingly strained, particularly over a deal called the Walking Purchase of 1737. This ceded land to the colonists as far as men could walk in a day: the colonists selected fast runners. It seems someone read their ancient history and remembered the tale of the Philaeni brothers, the Carthaginians who took part in a competition against the Greeks to claim as much land as they could cover. In this instance, though, the winners weren't buried alive. Perhaps such an outcome might have eased diplomacy, as matters have gone downhill since then and you'll see few Indians in their old coastal lands, changing the landscape forever.

The Powhattans were another confederation that will be

recognisable from anyone familiar with the stories of the original Virginian settlements. Their power has now been broken and their extent diminished. The Monacans have shifted from their old grounds to become linked to the Iroquois. The names that were such a terror or a vital aid to the first settlers are now distant names or remnants of villages.

If you want to live life on the edge though, try tracking down one of the tribes on the frontiers. The Tuscarora Indians have been increasingly made hostile by colonists encroaching on their lands. North Carolina wisely stopped but then Virginians started. The Tuscorora War breaks their power and drives many of their number northwards to join the Iroquois grouping, so if you encounter a member at this stage do be aware of this back history.

The Catawba are named (by colonists) after their river valley. They have an even more fierce reputation, ensuring that the governors of South Carolina strive to keep on their good side even when they had been decimated by wave after wave of smallpox. You may hear about their chief, Hagler, who in 1763 brokers a deal for land title from the Crown. Sadly it's looking as if their numbers will mean leasing some of this land out, which will ultimately threaten their title to it.

The Cherokee tribes are another large grouping. They are largely friendly to the British until the Seven Years War, after which Georgian settlements in particular hit them too. Markedly, they sit more at a crossroads between neighbouring Indian groups. An important meeting point is their key tribal meeting place known as the Centre of the World. Mind the trees as you visit to trade; they are prime roosting spots for countless masses of migrating passenger pigeons. Bring a disposable hat.

Next door are the Creeks, who remain the majority population in Georgia until well into the eighteenth century. Initially, the colonists exchanged metalware and textiles for slaves (supplied, unwillingly, by Florida Indians), which was subsequently replaced by the deerskin trade for export to English clothiers. So it is quite possible that as you read this bound book, kicking off your fine leather boots, you are already unknowingly familiar with their materials. The Creeks largely stay neutral in 1776, trade weakens, and so do their prospects as settler expansionism becomes more abrupt.

We advise you to steer clear of the Seminoles, a Creek tribe associated with the Spanish. Encroachment on the Spanish territories of Florida is also an encroachment on their lands. They may only number perhaps over a thousand, but it should be sufficient to reflect that their name comes originally from what the Spanish called them - cimarrones, or free people.

Across in the Mississippi region, the tribe you'll hear about is the Choctaw. These too are old French allies. From 1801 and the Treaty of Fort Adams, it's clear that the US Government is seeking to buy up the rights to their vast land on a massive scale.

Further inland we expect you won't be inclined to go, and we have even less of an understanding of their strange and savage ways that lie far from any decent tailor or the prospect of sorbet. Those concerned with trade in the factories of the far north could profitably study the manners of the local peoples who are not of Indian stock. The Esquimaux live in the desolate regions of snow and tundra. They call themselves the Innuit (the men), and they call Europeans the Kaublunet. They eat deer, salmon, seals, whales, birds, and cod, and catch herring with small nets. They have canoes called kaiaks, and harpoons which are connected by cords to air bladders that float on the surface and mark the location of wounded prey at sea. They have hunting dogs. Note that they can be concerned by how visiting Europeans are proving untoward with their women, so yours may not be a welcome presence. If you do get to stay with them, be prepared to eat a lot of boiled foodstuffs, including dogs and whale heads.

Those Esquimaux with less contact with Europeans probably won't be able to tell the difference between you and a Frenchman, even in full uniform. But if you bring something they need then that's what counts. We recommend files, saws, cutting tools (perhaps visit a shoe maker for these), knives, pewterware, fishing tools (forget the rods), cooking pots, and bright beads for the women.

Indian Customs

It would be a mistake to ascribe common processes across all these peoples, whose various climates, histories, settings, contacts with Europeans, and language links have generated many different manners and lifestyles. Let us here flag up merely a handful that you may explore all the more eagerly.

Dance is rather a different affair than back home. Music is more basic, with a potential monotony that can be quite hypnotic and accompanied by some garbled chant. If the whole group is joining in, you may be encouraged to too. We would encourage polite discretion and enquiry rather than just leaping in, just in case your randomly invertebrate shaking, twitching and hopping is deemed offensively inappropriate to some shamanic ritual.

The reverence given to storytelling is reminiscent of our own ancient past. You may not be able to follow the tale (sitting next to an interpreter before it starts might be a sagacious move), but you'll tangibly feel the audience get wrapped up in the tension.

The Indians are also celebrated for superstitious magical displays. Try to take these calls for supernatural assistance in the spirit that they are intended - excuse the pun - or at least avoid openly demonstrating puritanical disdain for their beliefs (unless you are a vicar).

The Cherokee and Creek, who have long lived in the tobacco regions, are known for their peace pipes. This may be baked clay, or possibly of local stone, and its bearer is treated with the respect due to an ambassador. Make sure it is a peace pipe though, and not a war pipe if your local tribe uses one of those as well. The error could be embarrassing.

No doubt as the western hinterland becomes more explored, the tribal customs of the plains Indians will become more familiar to us also.

Scalping does exist and is a longstanding Indian custom. But note also there is a strong tendency for frontiersmen to adopt this practice too, along with so many other ways of wilderness living, so one can hardly accuse just the savages of savagery. The act is considerably frowned upon by gentlemen of all nationalities, including the French, and officers generally attempt quite rightly to dissuade their Indian allies from this degrading custom - at least as concerns European victims. Scalps are usually, but not always, taken from the dead. The Iroquois exhibit them at home, stretched out by hoops, acting as symbolic replacements to their own tribes people lost in battle. But from a European perspective, the value lies more in proving that the 'British' Indian has killed a 'French' Indian and therefore confirms a claim for payment.

Indians, and to some extent French Canadians who occasionally dress and act like them, have a reputation for treating their prisoners badly - which we would define by torture and murder rather than accepting an officer's parole and offering them tea.

The details involved are, frankly, too horrible to share in polite society. Suffice it to say that what bits could be carved up or off when tied to a tree, can be.

Even corpses are not sacrosanct. Tales of skinning by Indians and of Indians adds an enduring and horrible aspect to fighting alongside or against them, though perhaps no different from the macabre relics occasionally seen back home that have been plucked off the corpses of hanged highwaymen and murderers.

So the basic rule is not to get captured in the woods; and if you really must surrender, speedily find a European officer who might be able to protect you. The second rule is not to panic when you hear someone whooping, because the worst thing you can do is have everyone on your side also just running around screaming. The third rule is yourself to pretend you have some very angry Indians with you, to better spook the enemy. Practise your war cry in your spare time, preferably though when your friends are not playing whist in the next room.

Survival Tips

The greatest explorers of the hinterland, especially the Scotsmen who have done most to develop trade routes in Canada, pay due respect to what they have learned from the native peoples. Having lived on the land for so long, despite their access to advanced technology such as the lathe and the spinning jenny, they have developed improvised ways to make key equipment from bare materials whose efficiency would astound a woodsman in the counties.

A book can't tell you enough - you'll have to learn it by watching the masters. But consider for instance the various uses that a dead animal can be put to, from providing the hides to provide for clothing or tents, to making tools from bones for hunting or sewing, to the sinews that supply the threads to hold everything together. Similarly, trees can produce more than firewood or permanent housing - which is far from practical if you are on the move chasing scant resources. Bark can provide the base materials for transport (the canoe), the waterproof material for a water container, a nutritious flavouring for an arboreal brew, or even the glue to bind items together.

Indian Trade

Remember to consider what the particular tribes need as well as what they can supply. Clearly, pelts are portable and relatively high value for what they weigh, plus they carry a major mark up for any middleman, though note that supplies will over time dwindle as sources become over used and either you or the trapper may have to travel further to find them. Once trade routes develop with trappers in the Pacific west, sea otter pelts will go for a fortune on the Chinese market.

Practical metal items are safe bets for bartering. Forget paper notes entirely. Even coins are a distraction in the wilds far from any colonial village that might accept them. Muskets, flints, gunpowder, and steel blades can all find a market. It has been said though that the last sight of many a killed settler has been a tomahawk coming towards him with Made in Sheffield marked on the side.

An Iroquois warrior in his dancing regalia. Remember to bring your party clothes.

It's crucial here to be aware of legal limits on trading alcohol with the natives. A number of colonies have legislation curtailing it so be cautious you stick to what the law allows for. An Act of Massachussetts Bay from 1693 gives a good idea of what you can expect. It forbids the sale of strong beer, ale, cider, perry (pear cider), wine, rum, brandy and other spirits. The fine is a huge disincentive at

40/- (forty shillings) per pint sold, and two months in jail if you can't pay. Note though there are exceptions for providing one or two drams as an act of charity, in case of sickness or fainting, if a physician provides authority in writing or a JP so orders. Drunk Indians themselves are subject to a 5/- fine and up to ten lashes.

Making Preparations

What to Bring

It's likely that you will be seeking to make landfall at one of the principal ports. This means that you will be able to make up any shortfall in possessions on arrival. You will, however, have to make allowances as high range items are imported. Thus if you are after a fur coat for instance you may find it less expensive and more stylish to buy one before departure, even if the fur originally came from the other side of the Atlantic! If you are seeking tailored silks you can be expected to pay a major premium for having accompanied the goods across the ocean.

That said, basic winter accessories can be readily obtained at your destination, so there should be no need to pack snow shoes and skates. If you plan to travel a lot rather than loiter in the capitals, ensure that you bring rugged travel clothes - there is nothing more embarrassing that leaving your shoe buckle in the stage coach. Pistols are more practical than sword canes in a setting where tomahawks are increasingly a weapon of choice, even amongst officers in the field. Expect fashion to be anywhere from six months to a generation behind the times.

Those who have taken a leave of absence from style over the past few years might profitably acquaint themselves with a few terms. A banyan is a form of informal attire that resembles a night gown or Moroccan single-piece long shirt. Breeches cover the upper legs, and leggings the lower, while a long shirt and waistcoat - especially the waistcoat, never be without it - do the rest. Those looking to blend in, or purchase mementos of their stay, could look for an authentic American hunting shirt which is a rugged and personalised affair. Trousers are a bit common, or betray a background in the Navy.

Coats over the century become shorter. Better protection from the elements can be found in the cloak, or increasingly the great coat. Some sort of neck covering, or cravat, is essential.

Most people of substance wear wigs. Coming from or through London, it's possible yours might provoke interest as being of the latest fashion. You will likely find it difficult to perch your hat on top. For much of this period you may be carrying your tricorne or three-pointed hat rather than wearing it. Walking sticks and canes are optional and of limited practical value in more rural contexts, except for knocking on doors.

Visas

As a British subject arriving on a British ship, you are unlikely to be vexed by issues of paperwork while going about your personal business. It will become more of an issue during hostilities, but even after independence we can scarcely find much need for you to obtain a travel document, considering how open the society is. No doubt the Foreign Secretary, who has to personally sign each one, is relieved.

As an officer you might simply elect to carry with you the paperwork confirming your Commission.

Travelling Safely

Driving

A gentleman never drives his own coach. Many people walk, though that hardly suits either, particularly if there are distances involved. Horses suit, particularly when moving along less travelled routes where road surfaces may be less than exemplary.

The Conestoga wagon, originally native to Pennsylvania, is a form of heavy goods transport and is inappropriate - you can spot them as they often have awnings peculiarly stretched forwards and backwards at the top, and floors that slope upwards to keep the contents from shifting.

Stage coaches can be found through most of the century. Do not expect the standard to reach that of England. Seating is basic. Enter via the front rather than any side door. Try to get in first so you have a back rest, or be prepared in company to surrender this seat to a lady. Wrap up warm.

Toll roads or turnpikes are starting to appear here in the Low Season, so bring loose change.

The conestoga wagon, as it is called, is a favorite of farmers in New England. It is capacious, strong and the canvas cover protects goods from the elements.

Highwaymen

It's not just England that has to deal with the likes of Dick Turpin. He has his counterparts here too. Some are simple river pirates preying on vessels plying the Mississippi. The open roads of the underpopulated West also appear to be a growing zone of opportunity for organised gangs, so beware of fellow travellers who might exploit the trust you have loaned them after several days of acquaintance.

A classic case is that of Thomas Mount. A thief and serial deserter (from both sides) during the War of Independence, he goes on to rob his way across the east coast via the odd escaped cell or two. During his final incarceration, he reveals the background to a society of villains and highwaymen known as the Flash Company. They have their own jargon (like thieves in medieval France) and even like pirates have their own songs. Whether it's an accurate portrayal or a way of gleaning attention from the public is a matter of conjecture. We would counsel you travelling with a loaded pistol to be on the safe side.

Off Road

Do not go off road when away from the coastal areas. The forests are wild and huge. Tracks are sparse and easy to lose. You could travel for days without seeing a soul, and without foraging skills you will starve and die.

If you really must, ensure you have an impeccable sense of direction, sufficient water skins, and a hunting rifle. A compass, affixed for instance to your walking stick, is an essential tool. Avoid unnecessary expeditions in the winter. There is a reason why the army does not campaign until the eve of spring. Do not be picky: adapt to local habits to survive.

Health and Insurance

Generally speaking, you will find the New World setting as a gentleman less rigorous than life in London. Diseases do abound though, particularly in the more southerly climes where Malaria and Yellow Fever are both killers. Even Philadelphia is not safe, suffering a terrible bout of the latter in 1793 and killing perhaps a tenth of the population.

Small Pox has been a wider threat, and is particularly devastating to the Indians who have limited resistance. Indeed, there has been occasional talk of attempting to use it as a deliberate weapon of war against them. Even amongst Europeans, the fatality rate is perhaps around one in five. One developing option is whether or not to attempt to inoculate using a mild infection. This is fiercely debated, since inoculation is not without serious risk. As the century progresses, royal example and proven immunity means opposition has largely diminished. The results of subsequent research that has been ongoing in England, looking at using the safer cow pox vaccine, is anticipated with interest.

Consumption (Tuberculosis) is showing an increase, but perhaps due to rather different urban conditions and an absence of patients to spread it (whatever its cause) it is not yet so marked. That may change as immigration brings in those suffering from it.

Healthcare is as good as your access to local doctors, which may be patchy. However, thanks in part to Mr Benjamin Franklin (whose good works repeatedly crop up in this tome), as of 1751 the colonies gain its first proper hospital in Pennsylvania. It is also, though this is hopefully not of use to you, an insane asylum. It is worthy of note that in this the French have a head start owing to their charitable orders. The order that would in time become known as the Grey Nuns of Montréal branch out from a house for the poor (set up in 1737) to take over the city's hospital in 1747. The Hôpital Général had been set up in 1692 but had fallen financially into hard times. The nuns will play a great role in helping the city through the smallpox epidemic of 1755. Perhaps it's more of a hospice that a medical establishment but it's a valuable first port of call for travellers in difficulties. In Québec, its counterpart was founded in 1692 and is run by a minor order of friars.

Life insurance is an option you may wish to take out, to accompany any merchandise insurance to cover loss during shipping (there are two authorised ones - try Mr Lloyd's coffee house) or at fire risk in the warehouse. This is best achieved before departure at London, the world's insurance capital. Do be conscious that turnover of companies is relatively high, but these tend not to cover international trade anyhow. If you are under 45, turn to the Amicable Society; if over, and it is after 1762, the Society for Equitable Assurances on Lives and Survivorships has an expanded remit.

Compensation for personal accidents, steam boiler explosions, and burglary do not yet exist.

Witchcraft

The colonies have moved on substantially since the Salem Witch Trials, now seen as an aberration. A successful prosecution does crop up in Norfolk in 1705, and a small number of others also lead to acquittals and damages.

One shouldn't rule it out entirely but society is largely of a mind not to prosecute even obvious cranks who might think they have special powers. It would, though, be bad form to start accusing people of owning malevolent familiars even in jest.

The Salem Witch Trials were a few years ago now, but although civilised opinion has moved on it is best not to wear a pointy hat and stroke a black cat in more rural areas.

Food and Drink

Food

While you are here you should take the opportunity to taste local products and dishes. Some you will be familiar with as it is either exported (like Newfoundland cod) or a local variant of a traditional British dish. Fish is particularly common in New England, sited as it is near such rich grounds.

You're less likely to be familiar with pemmican. This is of Indian origin, and is a form of cake made from a mix of meat paste and berries which is good travelling fare. Indeed, dried beef is a commonplace. So too are oats dishes amongst settlers of Scottish origin.

Okra is an African plant that followed the slave trade, used as a seasoning for instance in a stew accompanied by mullet or rice, or put into a seafood soup to make gumbo. Turkeys are a popular catch, so much so in fact that the population of the various species is suffering a disastrous decline. These are wild game and should not be confused with the farmed guinea fowl from back home.

Scrapple is a Pennsylvanian dish, made up of pork or beef scraps mixed with cornmeal. Clabber is sour milk which can be used in making cakes. Game is obviously very popular in the countryside; on the plains that essentially means bison, which tastes like a thin beef. Turtles provide eggs or the basis for a soup; indeed, the flavour changes depending on which part of the turtle you use. For greens, there is an array of peculiar local vegetables from which to draw. Passenger Pigeons are so common that they are an easy addition to the menu.

Try out some variety in those areas that have some French influence. Traditional French Canadian food often seems to include the popular staple of maple syrup, for instance as a flavouring for a sugary and creamy pie. Tourtière by contrast, is a spicy meat pie. You may find others referred to as pâtés. Pea soup is a common and easy dish. Pork is a popular commoner's offering, and you can find some decent cheeses (especially if you like curds). Duck's another option.

Over in Prince Edward Island, the potatoes have a good reputation, and so too do the mussels. Nova Scotian seafood, including the lobster, matches the best New England has to offer. Newfoundland has adopted screech, a Jamaican rum aged locally, as a favourite.

In short, you'll have plenty of opportunity to experiment with the finest local produce. Some tastes you'll have to leave behind. Pears and cherries for instance are yet to be widely introduced from Europe. As compensation, blueberries offer an easy crop to pickers and you can find wild raspberries and strawberries, the former peculiarly in both black and red.

Drink

Unless there's an embargo on, you should be able to enjoy Europe's customary exported wines. The commoner material is brewed locally. That means largely ale, though cider is in some places a popular alternative now that apple trees have been brought over. Barley is largely imported, though this is beginning to change and hops grow wild, which has encouraged rural householders to brew their own.

Be aware of the politics surrounding hot beverages when you place an order.

Planning Your Visit

Public holidays

Bear in mind that there are certain days where business may be constrained. Naturally there is Christmas. A localised phenomenon is Thanksgiving, which is an opportunity for a social gathering such as perhaps a meal to commemorate an event of some current or past significance. For example, there is one to remember the first harvest reaped by the Plymouth colony which you'll find commemorated in Massachusetts; but the events recalled vary dependent on the local history.

The religious festivals you may be used to back home have in many cases here faded away. Beware of attempting to exploit St Valentine's Day in particular. Forget May Day, and don't expect pancakes. Candlemas is still remembered, but a handful of Pennsylvanians are rumoured to associate it with checking to see if some peculiar rodent pokes its head out of the ground.

On the other hand, election days are treated as public holidays, and the halting of Guy Fawkes's activities is still commemorated in New England. Days designated for militia drilling may also impact.

From the middle of the century, you might also find yourself in the midst of what locals call a "Negro Election Day", where this community gathers to elect governors and kings. Slaves are given the day off to celebrate in a series of social events and games, with owners even ensuring they are properly attired. It reminds one of the Roman festival of the Saturnalia with a role reversal of society. Predictably, the Southern colonies treat this with the deepest suspicion.

The Calendar

Remember that Britain follows the Julian Calendar, at least until 1752. This will mean you jump around three months forward when crossing into neighbouring foreign colonies that use the Gregorian system. Adjust cross-border social diaries accordingly.

The wild turkey fowl is a favourite game bird for the locals who eat it in prodigious quantities.

Sundays

The Sabbath is followed less, well, puritanically than in the past, but do be aware that it is generally considered a day of rest. This means that trading may well be one of the "blue laws" in the colony, that is to say legislation that bans certain activities on holy days. The term is said to come from the paper the puritans wrote them on, though the expression appears of less certain origin on review.

Also be prepared potentially to be invited to socialise at the houses of fellow church-goers after the service.

Opening Hours

Expect working days to run from sunrise to sunset.

Accommodation

As in Britain, you will stop over in taverns. These are social focal points for the local community, and a good place to pick up news and gossip while supping a home-made ale. You can also dine here.

Quality varies massively. Accepted clientele also varies. You may find particularly notoriously rowdy groups, such as sailors and Indians, banned by law. Slaves will also often be excluded.

Toilets

We are not optimistic of swift universal adoption of the various water closet advances undertaken in the 1770s by Messrs Cumming (S trap), Prosser (plunger closet) and Bramah (crank valve and cistern float), or Gaitland's water trap U bend of 1782. Expect to be disappointed, and carry something scented.

Chapter 2
The Politics of Revolt

It is our duty to acquaint your Lordship that on the 4th July last the General Congress came to a Resolution to declare that the associated colonies are and of right ought to be free and independent states, that they are absolved from all allegiance to the British Crown and that all political connection between them and the state of Great Britain is and ought to be totally dissolved. A printed copy of the Declaration of Independence came accidentally to our hands a few days ago after the dispatch of the Mercury Packet and we have the honor to inclose it.

Report of the Howe brothers from Staten Island, 11 August 1776

Grievances (and Redress)

The Americans who complain about taxes really don't know how lucky they are. As someone who has come over from England, you will be aware of the crippling levels of debt that the country is in. By the close of the Seven Years War, Britain has had to pay for the War of the Spanish Succession, the War of the Austrian Succession, bailing out the South Sea Company which went calamitously bust and threatened to ruin the economy, plus the recent conflict which was fought all over the entire world. In addition to fighting the French to protect Hanover (with only the Prussians as our allies, against Austria, Russia, Sweden and France), warfare has been going on in India, Cuba, the Philippines, and Africa, not counting the huge costs of the conflict in North America. The country is flat broke, and ordinary folk are being taxed to the hilt to service the debts let alone pay them off.

In that context, asking the colonists to contribute should not seem excessive, especially when the sums involved are so low. There may be four times as many British subjects back home, but we are as a community across the board paying ten times what the colonists are. It gets worse when you look at individual rates of taxation. Some calculate that on average, the typical British taxpayer is paying 26/- (shillings) a year in taxes, while a colonist is paying just 1/-

Much of this was spent to protect them from the French and the Indians. The French are no longer a threat; the Indians are, so the colonists need garrisons. Someone has to pay for them, and why should it be us?

Now it's true that Pitt during the Seven Years' War stepped in to help a number of the colonies who had low revenues, to pay for the troops they were raising to help the regulars go off to the front. That was key to getting them to agree to raise colonial militias. But should that even have had to happen in the first place?

We might put it another way. Watch how taxes go up after independence. Even during the revolution, see how inflation strikes and prices go through the roof as Congress breaks London's rule against printing money thoughtlessly. The result is an attempt to control prices, which doesn't work. The result in turn is the army can't or won't buy goods at the inflated market rate, and the end result of that is starvation and enduring the bitter cold at Valley Forge.

In July of 1775, the revolutionaries attempt to justify their activity by a declaration. In it, they claim that Parliament is "blinded" by an "intemperate rage for unlimited domination," and yet Parliament has repealed most of the legislation it had passed prior to Boston approaching a state of revolt. It had indeed introduced taxes, but on goods coming from and going to Britain. It had suspended trial by jury, but only because juries were either politicised or pressured into letting felons off for acts of piracy, and trials had simply been moved instead into neutral settings. Even under these supposed tyrannical conditions, the rights of the individual are greater than exist in the home towns of the Europeans who would come to support the revolutionaries.

The whole thing, you might think, is a farce. But you would be unwise to blindly enter upon such an assertion as the 1770s progresses, as sympathies are aroused for what you might privately be thinking of as the intransigent vandals of Massachusetts.

Troublemakers

As a loyal subject, you obviously already have a fixed perception of the rights and in particular the wrongs of the more noxious pamphleteers. You may be inclined to voice your opinions in a place like Boston. Consequently, the sorts of people you might expect to provoke as a social set will be the following;

* Traders who are vexed at being banned from smuggling;

* Traders annoyed at the attempt to sell cheap tea to the public rather than being able to sell their (quite possibly smuggled) tea;

* Those polarised by the stamp tax finding they now have to pay extra for legal bills, taking on crown roles, arranging land documents, or even buying a deck of playing cards (unfortunately, a significant number);

* Social malcontents;

* Revolutionaries and anti-monarchists;

* The ill-informed, for instance someone who has not read what the law on garrisoning troops actually is;

* The misinformed, especially over the propaganda relating to the somewhat immoderately-named "Boston Massacre";

* Nervous slave owners watching how English law is changing;

* Those considering any legal response to the above to be excessive, however restrained it might be;

* Lunatics, blackguards, and Frenchmen.

But this is far from the full story by a long chalk. To these we may notably add a number who have a genuine concern about the political evolution of the colonies and seek to establish due and proper form, so that abuses do not take place at the hands of an emerging east coast elite. We must also admit that the Bill of Rights is a relatively recent invention and protection.

Some taxes do seem peculiar, and some grievances genuine. For instance, colonial sailors are forced to contribute to pay for the upkeep of Greenwich Hospital several thousand miles away. Others have been impressed to sail on HMS Romney. Writs of Assistance are being used in a sweeping way to search property for smuggled goods, an approach deemed legal by English Courts but challenged in many American ones. The new Vice Admiralty Courts are based in far-off Halifax, geographically central in terms of the Atlantic but not in terms of the Thirteen Colonies. There has even been talk of establishing the Church of England in America, which runs counter to everything non-conformists hold dear. These are genuine concerns that should obviously be addressed.

Unfortunately, this group, while very large, is not as loud as the above.

Attempts at Mediation

America becomes polarised in the 1770s, but the situation is not without hope. An outstanding opportunity arises in 1774 with an idea set out by a Pennsylvanian delegate by the name of Joseph Galloway. He proposes a central grand council that would act as a continental parliament in areas that concerned more than one colony. Representatives would be elected, and the Speaker would be appointed by the King and would hold power of veto. It would be distinct from Parliament and Westminster, and both could veto the other. Tragically, this gets defeated by a single vote thanks to news arriving just at that very moment of escalating tensions in Boston. This is, we might suggest, perhaps the most disastrous near-miss in world history.

Even that is quite not the end. Parliament proposes a plan whereby the tax on colonial trade would be limited to provisioning for defence and to managing trade, which would have been eminently fair and astonishingly equitable. However, fighting had already broken out. As of 1775 there is very mixed messaging coming out between the colonial hardliners openly pushing for a break, and those who are pushing what is called the Olive Branch Petition and looking for a de-escalation. Ironically, these continuing feelers for peace (whether genuinely sought by some of those who profess it is difficult to judge) contribute to saving the Revolutionary army.

Cornered on Long Island, Washington's forces have been defeated. The Staten Island Peace Conference (11 September 1776) brings the British Peace Commissioners (the two Howe brothers, in charge of British forces) together with rebel delegates. Major General Sullivan, who had just been captured, has been released to take Congress an invite and a fuller acquaintance of the facts. Adams, Franklin and Rutledge are sent. But they are effectively demanding recognition as an independent state and so the terms are instantly unacceptable.

So it is all too late. Congress had by now already formally declared independence; it further makes the mistake of believing Admiral Howe's negotiating remit is narrower than it is; and the war party has meanwhile been trumpeting that it is just a ploy to divide rebels to better crush them.

The one actual result of the meeting may have been to discourage the British from taking the opportunity to rigorously pursue Washington and destroy the American field army utterly. His cornered force escapes Long Island, though a large key garrison does fall prisoner. Yet in political terms, the opportunity for a peaceful settlement is lost; now it can only come offered from a position of strength, and though the battlefields of 1777 come close the year doesn't quite provide.

In 1778, the Carlisle Commission tries again. This follows in the wake of a rather belated repeal of the Tea Act and of the legislation targeting Massachusetts. But it also follows British defeat at Saratoga, and more importantly it comes after the French have decided to intervene, and just as the British are demonstrating their weakness by preparing to pull out of Philadelphia. While the Commission is now offering self-rule within the British Empire, the revolutionaries are themselves set on getting the full package. A final attempt by the field commanders in 1781, conceding on all points short of independence, meets with no more success. The end deal that will be reached in Paris is full independence, pure and simple.

"I acquainted them that the king's desire to restore the public tranquillity, & to render his American subjects happy in a permanent Union with Great Britain, had induced him to constitute commissioners upon the spot to remove the restrictions upon trade & intercourse, to dispense the royal clemency to those who had been hurried away from their allegiance, to receive representations of grievances & to discuss the means whereby that mutual confidence & just relation which ought to subsist between the Colonies & the Parent State might be restored and preserved. [.../...]

"The three Gentlemen were very explicit in their opinions, that the associated Colonies would not accede to any Peace of Alliance, but as free & independent states, & they endeavoured to prove that Great Britain would desire more extensive & more durable advantages from such an alliance, than from the connexion it was the object of the Commission to restore. Their arguments not meriting a serious attention, the conversation ended, & the gentlemen returned to Amboy."

Lord Howe's account of the Staten Island Peace Conference

Cities, Colonies and Support

There are two main groups of political activists. Revolutionaries call themselves Patriots or Whigs. These call their opponents, the Loyalists, Tories. Whigs and Tories are names borrowed from the British political scene reflecting how radical or otherwise the party is.

When fighting breaks out with revolutionaries, many British officers will refuse to serve, considering themselves drawn into a civil war against their fellows. This triggers a need to deploy mercenaries from Germany, which the Patriot propagandists will exploit to the fullest.

Similarly though, it is important to note that local support for these wayward anarchists is far from universal, and geographically splintered.

The heartland of the revolt is Massachusetts, where the increasing strictures intended to control and punish the recalcitrant has tended rather to stiffen their backs. Virginia has a large number of the so-called Patriots. Across New England they are a dominant political force and outnumber their opponents. These occupy major centres of colonial settlement. But they do not mean a universal majority, since there are a large number of undecideds, pacifists, profiteers, or people who understandably feel caught in the middle and who want to steer clear.

By contrast, the numbers of those supporting the Crown - the Loyalists - may be as high as four in ten, certainly at rates of one in three. These numbers are stiffened as revolutionary mobs start to run amok, destroying peoples' homes, threatening to murder clergymen, forming vigilante groups to assassinate and intimidate, stripping people naked and covering them in tar, or making them 'ride the rails' (sitting astride a painful bar). Such excesses by mob rule are condoned by the revolutionary leadership.

That makes a million souls who still support the Crown even at the low water mark. While we cannot be certain as there is no census, they seem to form the majority in New Jersey, Pennsylvania, the Carolinas and Georgia. Of the key cities, both New York and Philadelphia have a strong reputation for Loyalism, as does Norfolk (until at least it is evacuated in late 1775 and burned in a fire fight). Even in areas of strong revolutionary zeal, they emerge to join up once the rebels have been ousted.

One dividing line is religion, with Loyalists tending often to be Anglicans (and revolutionaries Presbyterians). They are often from wealthier classes, from which we might suggest they are better educated. Sometimes they are of recent arrival, particularly the Scots. Around 30,000 are sufficiently motivated to enrol in His Majesty's forces, despite terror threats to their homes and families - burnings or tarring and feathering. Around 100,000 feel sufficiently aggrieved by the Revolution, or targeted as opponents of it, that they leave the new United States to resettle elsewhere. That's an astonishing five per cent of the population that leaves.

The Text of the Proclamation of Rebellion

(By which the British Government recognises treason is officially afoot)

"Whereas many of our subjects in divers parts of our Colonies and Plantations in North America, misled by dangerous and ill designing men, and forgetting the allegiance which they owe to the power that has protected and supported them; after various disorderly acts committed in disturbance of the publick peace, to the obstruction of lawful commerce, and to the oppression of our loyal subjects carrying on the same; have at length proceeded to open and avowed rebellion, by arraying themselves in a hostile manner, to withstand the execution of the law, and traitorously preparing, ordering and levying war against us: And whereas, there is reason to apprehend that such rebellion hath been much promoted and encouraged by the traitorous correspondence, counsels and comfort of divers wicked and desperate persons within this realm: To the end therefore, that none of our subjects may neglect or violate their duty through ignorance thereof, or through any doubt of the protection which the law will afford to their loyalty and zeal, we have thought fit, by and with the advice of our Privy Council, to issue our Royal Proclamation, hereby declaring, that not only all our Officers, civil and military, are obliged to exert their utmost endeavours to suppress such rebellion, and to bring the traitors to justice, but that all our subjects of this Realm, and the dominions thereunto belonging, are bound by law to be aiding and assisting in the suppression of such rebellion, and to disclose and make known all traitorous conspiracies and attempts against us our crown and dignity; and we do accordingly strictly charge and command all our Officers, as well civil as military, and all others our obedient and loyal subjects, to use their utmost endeavours to withstand and suppress such rebellion, and to disclose and make known all treasons and traitorous conspiracies which they shall know to be against us, our crown and dignity; and for that purpose, that they transmit to one of our principal Secretaries of State, or other proper officer, due and full information of all persons who shall be found carrying on correspondence with, or in any manner or degree aiding or abetting the persons now in open arms and rebellion against our Government, within any of our Colonies and Plantations in North

America, in order to bring to condign punishment the authors, perpetrators, and abetters of such traitorous designs.

Given at our Court at St. James's the twenty-third day of August, one thousand seven hundred and seventy-five, in the fifteenth year of our reign.

GOD save the KING."

Spotting Loyalists

Loyalists are not slavishly blind to their mother country's faults. They may even oppose recent policy, just as many supporters of the Royalist cause a century earlier had been strong critics of Charles I before fighting began. But just as the radicals are delighted at the prospect of independence rather than negotiation, so too are the moderate critics horrified and driven into opposing them. Taking an extreme position pushes others into taking either extreme as well.

Like in the 1640s, politics can divide families. Benjamin Franklin we know of as a revolutionary, albeit perhaps a guarded one. His son, Sir William Franklin, is not only governor of the Jerseys but a stalwart of the Crown who prefers exile.

You can generally spot one of the King's Men by their willingness to toast George III. More likely, they might use something along the following lines: "My country, may she always be right; but right or wrong, my country."

This social description may not serve you well on campaign. Consider the lot of Major André. He was travelling from "above", ie from rebel lines in those parts, to "below", that is to say British lines. Approaching the latter, he was taken prisoner (and later executed) by some Patriot soldiers who appeared initially to be on his side.

An early indicator of how things will turn out is with the tests. This begins with the army test, the requirement for all able-bodied male adults in revolutionary areas to sign up to the militia, which by definition means commitment to fight against (as Loyalists would see it) the lawful government. Then come the test laws. Such residents are required after 1776 to drop their former allegiance to the Crown and swear a new oath to their local government. Refusal means they do not go on the list of oath-takers, and do not get a certificate protecting them from arrest. Refusal opens up the prospect of arrest and worse. As it happens, the death sentence that's on the books tends not to get carried out, though it may have given the French some ideas later, and there are infamous exceptions including the executions of two Philadelphian Loyalists hanged for their politics. More commonly, Loyalists are taxed punitively (ironic, given the cause of the revolt); their property is stolen by the state; their legal rights and protections are removed. If travelling in Revolutionary areas, you can spot the Loyalist as he's the one being openly persecuted, including through serious assault. As of January 1777, Washington gives thirty days to all Loyalists in his lines who have signed up to Lord Howe's offer of a pardon to leave, after which they are to be considered enemies.

Naturally, what comes around, goes around. With the frontier fighting in the north turning on Indian-style raids and the fighting in the Carolinas centring on Loyalist regiments, it is inevitable that terrible atrocities will happen. It speaks volumes that the Americans who seize the legislative chamber at York in 1813 on finding the Speaker's wig mistake it for an American scalp. A crime against fashion thus escalates. It's also telling that after Yorktown, Cornwallis is allowed a sloop to send news of his surrender, and that it is allowed to depart unchecked - which means he is able to smuggle his Loyalists away. It's an alarmingly informative recognition of what their lot will be, and possibly a pointer of connivance by Washington himself (and even he hated them).

So the Revolution is in truth a bitter civil war. The United States' loss ultimately is Canada's gain, though the end destinations of the exiled Loyalists in fact prove as varied as those expelled from Acadie. Many will settle in Nova Scotia or in Upper Canada, or form the Eastern Townships of Lower Canada. A number will include escaped slaves, including those who had worked as pioneers for the British army, and whom the British commander Sir Guy Carleton refuses to abandon at New York as a point of honour despite the insistence of the American leadership. Ultimately, some of these will in turn go on to colonise Sierra Leone.

The process of re-establishment is arduous, even with the support of the British Government that allows many former officials and soldiers to go on the books on half-pay, and with vast tracts of wilderness assigned to them. It will add several million Pounds to the country's hefty national debt to accommodate them. But from this time there also arises another mark of distinction that sets the Loyalists apart. In 1789, Carleton decides to create an honorific: to commemorate the work these people had done for their country, United Empire Loyalists would be allowed to affix the letters "U.E." after their name, an honour intended to be passed on to future generations. Eligible names are compiled on oath and written down for future record. So if you encounter those letters in the Low Season, you know you're in the company of a genuine old fashioned Loyalist or one of their descendants. Their homes are ruder, more basic, bereft of many of the fineries they have left behind. Their towns are recent, underdeveloped, lacking in modern technologies, and just plum bare compared with the years of development that had gone into what has been lost. But, by George, they are British.

A British newspaper cartoon shows Britannia welcoming the Loyalists - some places in America would not be so friendly.

"So far from having given the least countenance or encouragement to the most unnatural, unprovoked Rebellion that ever disgraced the Annals of Time, we have on the contrary steadily & uniformly opposed it in every stage of its Rise and Progress, at the Risque of our Lives and Fortunes."

Part of an address from inhabitants of New York, November 1776

Politics After Independence

Those travelling in the Low Season may find it of peculiar interest to observe how the politics of the former colonies have been developing. The most interesting period is when the US constitution is being worked out.

In sum, we might define matters as a division between two principal parties. These are the Federalists, and the Anti-Federalists. In essence, it boils down to a debate about how much power is needed by central government, as opposed to being left to the separate states to apply. With the removal of the former unifying authority - the British Crown - a vacuum has been formed and it is by no means certain which argument will win.

So what do the two groups in essence believe?

Federalists tend to support the development of trade links with Britain. They believe that a federal government should be relatively strong, to tie together the various states (especially any unruly ones), and to act as the lead protector of the individual. They support a standing federal army. They support the separation of powers between three different branches specifically as a defence against too strong a central government, since they too support the concept of states having some rights. They are concerned about having a Bill of Rights, since defining the rights central government is supposed to protect may allow it freedom to violate the others, and in any event since power is loaned by the states they have the ultimate right to take powers back anyhow.

Some call them more elitist, but if so that is because of an experience with how mob rule has worked out. They want federal courts under a Supreme Court, are after a federal tax-raising power, and seek to ensure trade across the states is even-keeled and avoids local protectionism. They support a large marine that competes with other merchant fleets, and are content to establish a small but powerful navy - enough ships of the line to tip the balance in any European war waged in the Caribbean, meaning that the country will be wooed with good trade terms rather than despised as weak.

Anti-Federalists in short support the masses ("the people") over the elite. They tend to lean more towards an association with France. They support the primacy of the states over any central government. As part of this, they support the idea of a bill of rights to protect the individual. They oppose a standing federal army, seeing it as a potential threat. They support a Bill of Rights, since state versions might be overridden by the Constitution. They do not approve of a large federal capital set apart in its own territory. They prefer annual elections, and constitutions to be ratified by every state rather than a two thirds majority. They also want reference to God kept in any constitution, and any powers over trade, law courts and tariffs kept out. They are worried about the future development of the role of the President.

The type of central government first set out in July 1776 is extraordinarily limited. It is barely enough to wage war. There are no central tax powers, just requests; there is no power to raise an army, just setting some requested quotas to be filled locally; there is not even any power to regulate internal commerce even when something has been agreed in an international treaty. All states get equal votes, despite major disparities. In 1781 as a result, tiny Rhode Island alone vetoes the introduction of a 5% import tax.

Could this endure? Some states benefit more than others from a stronger central government. Some suffer from social unrest; some are in debt; some face Indian threats; some have claims on western lands that central government might remove; some have efficient local government and see no need for change. The debate pits protectionist manufacturers against raw goods exporters; slave against non-slave states; small states against large.

Those looking for a swift introduction to the arguments could profitably turn to the series of essays known as the Federalist Papers, which argue their cause through a series of newspaper pieces over 1787-8 that are subsequently collected in book form. In turn, these triggered a number of responses from the other side.

Naturally, there are differences of opinion within each group. The authors of the Federalist Papers for instance (Hamilton, Madison and Jay) share the pseudonym of Publius, but occasionally differ on points, which will make interpreting intent more interesting for future generations of lawyers.

Anti-Federalists include those running under pseudonyms of their own, such as Brutus, Cato (George Clinton), Centinel, or Federal Farmer ('Harry' Lee).

What is astonishing is how the debate turns. In the Convention drafting the constitution, around two thirds are Anti-Federalists. Perhaps four sevenths of the population are. There is every reason to think that the states will remain largely disjointed, or may even form three or four small confederacies based on their common interests (perhaps uniting the four northern states, four middle, and five southern, with Pennsylvania supposedly becoming the "Flanders of America" as the contested hot spot for future conflicts between them).

But Anti-Federalists are by definition disjointed and uncentralised. They are thus defeated state by state without putting up a coordinated defence.

A central government is indeed formed. Yet the compromise reached is both revolutionary and an astonishingly productive one that actually looks as if it might work well.

These debates do become settled, and the arguments and arguers move on. As politicians take office in the new federal system there emerges a pro-administration group and an anti-administration group, which further develop into two political parties. Thus we have the Federalist Party of Mr Hamilton, and Mr Jefferson's party who are variously called Democrats, Republicans or Jeffersonians (take your pick).

If the United States explodes in an effervescence of political ideologies, rather the reverse happens with the remaining British colonies. The Lieutenant Governors administer the colonies, advised by councils of the social and administrative elite, members of the leading families who form the pinnacle of what passes for high society. True power, especially patronage, rests in the hands of the royal appointee.

Intriguingly, a challenge to this system is arising in Lower Canada though. The Quebec middle class is backing an emerging new political group, the Parti canadien. This gets its own newspaper in 1806, campaigning for more of a role by assembly members and more of a say by French Canadians in particular. Key leaders are then arrested, so democratic reform is in its very early stages yet.

The War of 1812

The Anti-Federalists sweep to power in the 1808 presidential elections. This puts a spoke in the wheel of Anglo-American relations. Key contentions are - whether the Royal Navy can board US ships to look for deserters, who undoubtedly exist; a number of genuine US nationals who end up impressed on British ships; whether Britain or for that matter France has a right in international law to seize neutral shipping such as that of the USA when trading with the enemy (Napoleon was the first to use this measure in the Berlin Decrees of 1806); the occasionally fettered access to the St Lawrence; British forts in the north west properly speaking on US territory; US maltreatment of and British support for certain Indian tribes; dreadful British diplomacy (helping the Federalists lose the last Presidential election); and unpaid US reparations to Loyalists from 1782.

But looming large was also the prospect of taking advantage of Britain being preoccupied by a massive war with Napoleon, and the prospect of a second attempt at a land grab that had failed four decades before. Could President Madison reunite the old British colonies by occupying the remainder under the US flag?

Identity

You might feel some sympathies with the American sailors faced down by what at first sight seem to be an oppressive Royal Navy. That might be so in some individual cases. But the reality is more complex.

Remember in your dealings with notional Americans that the laws and customs of the era do not lend themselves to fleet-footedness with respect to your national identity, simply because you have stepped foot in a foreign port. It's an issue that is crucial to understanding why runaway sailors are symbolic. Once a subject, one is always a subject. Impromptu defection while in the King's pay is also desertion.

The practices going on in American ports are also known to be nefarious and do not encourage a light response either. This is how Foreign Secretary Lord Castlereagh explains the situation – as a key cause of the war, it's worth quoting in depth;

"Nevertheless, so mitigated had been the conduct of his Majesty's government on the point in question, that the Admiralty had always directed our officers not to press seamen professing to be American-born who were found on board American vessels with certificates signed by the collector of the customs of an American port, and included in the certificated lists of the crew. It was, however, well known that these certificates were readily and fraudulently obtained, and granted to a degree perfectly inconsistent with any disposition on the part of the American government, and of the American officers, to counteract the abuse of which Great Britain complained. They were granted with a laxity which threw a deep stain on the character of the government of a country professing to rank among civilized nations. In two of the principal ports of America, New York and Philadelphia, the system of obtaining false certificates from the collectors was so disgracefully open, that in the former of those ports the collector one day allowed an old woman to qualify a whole host of seamen for receiving them, by swearing that she knew they were American citizens. The transaction proceeded to such a length that the very clerk remonstrated against its baseness, and appealed to the collector as to the possible credibility of the witness. The reply of the collector was, that it was no business of his, for that he was only ministerial in the affair; and the old woman continued during the whole of the day to receive her two dollars for every oath that she took, all who applied to her and through her means obtaining certificates. In Philadelphia, occurrences of a similar nature had taken place, but he would not fatigue the House by detailing them. Certificates were also frequently transferred from one individual to another, and became as much matter of sale as any other personal property. So much so indeed, that after a transfer of this kind it was no unusual thing to see produced by a person of colour, a certificate for his protection, describing him to be of fair complexion, light hair and blue eyes! But the question did not rest on this view of the fraudulent mode of granting and obtaining certificates. Was there not something in the practice of the American government which laid them open to a jealous suspicion on our part, even if the system of certificates was as faithful as

it was evidently fraudulent? Was there nothing to induce Great Britain not to part with the means of doing herself justice on the subject? Did America admit that the natural born subjects of this country were bound to give their aid and assistance to their natural sovereign? Her conduct distinctly denied it. She held that a British subject, who by a false oath converted himself into an American citizen, or who naturalized himself in America in conformity to the American laws, ceased to owe allegiance to the king of his native country, and was entitled to be protected as an American citizen. Contemplating all these circumstances, looking at the general spirit manifested by the government of the United States, looking at the known frauds of the certificating system, looking at the pretensions of the American legislature to divest, by Naturalization Bills, British subjects of their allegiance to their sovereign, so far from being encouraged to throw the point in question into the hands of the American government, it behoved this country to regard any such proposed surrender of their known and unalienable rights with jealousy, and to consult our own security before we gave up to America or to any other power the means which we possessed to defend ourselves, by the exercise of a right which never had been, and never could be, justly questioned."

ADDRESS RESPECTING THE WAR WITH AMERICA

HC Debate, 18 February 1813 vol 24 cc593-649

Two Views in Westminster

"Such are the causes of war which have been put forward by the government of the United States. But the real origin of the present contest will be found in that spirit, which has long unhappily actuated the councils of the United States: their marked partiality in palliating and assisting the aggressive tyranny of France; their systematic endeavours to inflame their people against the defensive measures of Great Britain; their ungenerous conduct towards Spain, the intimate ally of Great Britain; and their unworthy desertion of the cause of other neutral nations. It is through the prevalence of such councils, that America has been associated in policy with France, and committed in war against Great Britain."

DECLARATION OF HIS ROYAL HIGHNESS THE PRINCE REGENT RELATIVE TO THE CAUSES AND ORIGIN OF THE WAR WITH AMERICA.

HC Deb 03 February 1813 vol 24 cc363-77

Mr. Herbert (of Kerry) on the contrary was of opinion, that war with America ought to be avoided as much as possible. He had great doubts whether we were right in the present quarrel. As to what had been so much talked of,—our maritime rights,—he believed that much of what was claimed as maritime right, was somewhat doubtful. It appeared now, that we were to maintain those rights, as they were called, against almost all Europe. He hoped that those rights which were to be maintained against so formidable a force, would be just and clear beyond dispute. The policy of a war with America appeared to him to be as doubtful as the justice of it. It would cause an accession to France of many advantages in naval stores, and of a large body of sailors not inferior to our own.

Parliamentary Debate

HC Deb 13 February 1812 vol 21 cc762-801

Chapter 3
Information for Business Visitors

At present some of the States are little more than a society of husbandmen. Few of them have made much progress in those branches of industry which give a variety and complexity to the affairs of a nation.

Madison, The Federalist; Number 56 (1788)

Red tape

Trade interference is more of a French trait than a British one. Occasionally though you might find colonial assemblies passing laws that you need to be aware of, for instance keeping a limit on tobacco prices by limiting the amount that can be farmed per person.

After the Revolution you will find your markets not quite so open. US policy is becoming one of shifting away from supplying raw material to developing local manufactures. This doesn't happen immediately - indeed, the South prefers free trade for its products since it is still focused on exporting raw materials, and parts of New England are also so heavily linked in trade with Britain and Eastern Canada that they strongly oppose war in 1812. But when that war breaks out, the tariff goes up. After the war, British industrialists try to dump their produce cheaply to undercut their competitors, and the response to this is even higher tariffs. This appears now to be setting a trend that seems doomed to pit the contrasting needs of protectionist industrial north against agrarian free trade south.

Guilds

Do not expect to see the guild system with which merchants are so familiar over in Europe, and in particular London. Some do exist in the cities - particularly for areas involving carpentry, printing, and makers of certain parts of clothing – but when you consider that industry is not as developed as in England then it makes obvious sense that the professional organisations that accompany large bodies of specialist workers should be absent too. More importantly though, there is more work to be done than the manpower around to do it, which means the boundaries between various jobs is never enforced by professionals jealously keeping their competitors out. If somebody knows how to carve a plank and can do the job, what does it matter what the plank's used for so long as the job gets done?

The first recorded strike takes place by Philadelphia printers in 1786. Before then, you should find labour largely cooperative. After then, the workforce starts to become more organised. In 1806 there is a notable legal case between the government of Philadelphia and shoemakers, where a number of the latter are found guilty (though they only receive a small fine) for engaging on a criminal conspiracy to fix prices.

Local Government

Colonial government varies from place to place, since each colony was set up independently with different objectives and often by very different types of people. They may be overwhelmingly democratic; founded on a grant to a group or individual; or largely dependent upon royal governance. Royal colonies are increasingly taking over from private ones, though it must be pointed out that both have a vested interested in guaranteeing that assemblies do not have too many powers when it comes to taxes and finances.

The basic model consists of a central authority in the shape of the governor designated by the King, with advisers, and an assembly to provide consent. These are New Hampshire, Maryland, Rhode Island, the Carolinas, New Jersey, New York, and eventually the new settlement at Georgia.

Delaware shares a governor with, but has a separate assembly from, Pennsylvania. This latter has a large franchise, consisting of all free men who pay taxes.

Virginia has a representative government. It is a royal colony, but inherited an important assembly from the company whose charter was early revoked.

Massachusetts was established by merging two early colonies, Plymouth Colony and Massachusetts Bay. Plymouth's was originally set out in the Mayflower Compact, an agreement by the first settlers consenting to agree to what was decided communally. Massachusetts Bay has long had a two house legislative assembly.

Connecticut was largely the result of settlers moving in from Massachusetts. They brought with them a sense of representative democracy, which survives even now despite it being a crown colony. It has an early constitution in the shape of its Fundamental Orders, largely subsumed in its Royal Charter granted by Charles II. Famously, when James II/VII tried to abrogate it, the document was hidden away from his agents in an old white oak tree, the Charter Oak.

This means that there are different ideas on the extent to which ordinary people should be involved in local government, and who should elect or appoint them.

National Government

From 1686-1689, there was an attempt to unify many of these territories as the Dominion of New England. The territories were too diverse, and measures to simplify and centralise government were badly received. The fall of James II/VII swiftly encouraged the former colonial leaders to break up this failed experiment and re-establish their old institutions.

The idea re-emerges briefly in the 1750s, to increase cooperation against the French threat. It takes concrete form in the Albany Plan of 1754, whereby delegates from seven colonies agree to establish a Grand Council under a President General, raising taxes locally. While this would circumvent royal governors, it would also weaken local legislatures and as a result the concept does not get put into action.

A "Stamp Act Congress" does meet briefly in 1765, but this is more of a political plotting meeting intended to coordinate political opposition rather than run government. Also, not every colony is represented. It is far from revolutionary.

In any case, you will not see anything approaching a single colonial governing structure in his Majesty's territories. There is one, fatal, exception. The American Board of Customs is founded in 1767. Ostensibly, this is a sensible measure to ensure taxes are collected uniformly as the law requires, operating merely at the western end of the Atlantic rather than the eastern since British trade with Europe would carry different (indeed, higher) rates. Moreover, local agents have been so far removed from the London Board, there have been numerous complaints of inefficiency and abuse and this can now be reduced. Unhappily, the introduction at the same time of taxes on glass, lead, paper, tea and paint means that opposition to these gets lumped in with criticisms of reforms intended to improve accountability. It is doubly unfortunate that it's headquartered in Boston, the epicentre of discontent. From their very arrival the new Commissioners are treated with distrust and rising hostility, and in trying to do their job they start gradually to draw in military resources to a previously unmilitarised city.

The rest is (or will become) history. It is striking though that the first federal institution that gets set up by the independent United States is the Board's replacement.

However, some positions do carry universal authority, in particular individuals carrying commissions. The Commander in Chief, North America, enjoys universal military command and is of either Major General or Lieutenant General rank. The naval command, centred on Halifax or New York, is of a similar nature.

But if you are seeking to confer with an overarching power, you would be advised before arrival to arrange a guiding meeting on London (from 1768 onwards) with the Secretary of State for the Colonies. This is a role previously run from the office of the Secretary of State for the Southern Department, who largely covered Southern European diplomacy - the Spanish and Portuguese empires meant there was a New World relevance for this role. The new post also allows more focus than leaving matters in the overarching hands of the Board of Trade. You should be aware though that personal and departmental rivalries do significantly hamper policy making on America, sometimes getting in the way of good government.

Capitals of the United States

Uncertain where to find the leaders of the United States? They are in the capital city, of course. The problem is, over time it changes.

During the revolution when redcoats are running rampant, and before there is an established federal government, there are several sites where Congress meets. There's Philadelphia; Baltimore; Lancaster; and York (something there for students of the Wars of the Roses). Philadelphia is then supposed to be the set capital, but a mutinous army puts paid to that so off the government goes to Princeton; Annapolis; and also a brief visit to Trenton.

From 1785 New York becomes the capital. From 1790 it's centred on Congress Hall in Philadelphia. As quid pro quo for helping out with that state's debt, the capital shifts again to a stand-alone federal territory, and in late 1800 as the Capitol building becomes useable the seat of government is finally transferred over to Washington DC.

The City of Washington by the artist George Cook. Try not sneer at the capital city's small size, it won't go down too well.

Taxation

By and large, the British colonies are not terribly overtaxed. Where it becomes so, smuggling takes place. We do not endorse your joining their ranks as you do not enjoy any local support that might be roused, in mob form, by your competitors.

The Townsend Duties are those taxes which have been introduced, in part, to help defray the costs of government, and also to provide guaranteed salaries for colonial officials (in the process giving them independence from colonial assemblies). This means that at various times, certain import items will be taxed. Check timings before departure, though rates will not be prohibitive. Avoid importing tea during the period of the tea dispute as there is a local glut on the market, and your imports won't be offloaded anyway.

The basic rule to remember is that if you are trading, your first port of call should be the Customs House on arrival. Royal Navy cutters do patrol these waters and can quite legally board your vessel to ensure you are not dodging taxes.

A golden guinea of King George III. The king may not be popular everywhere, but good gold coin is.

Doing Business

Population

In Britain, the population has doubled over the last 500 years. In America, it doubles every 25 years. The denizens have a longer life and a better diet. They enjoy larger families, in part because more children survive, but also because large families are seen as a joy rather than as a burden. A young widow with several children is even courted rather than avoided. People marry young. Despite this there is an enduring scarcity of labour, resulting in increasing costs to hire people. This helps explain why people are keen to branch out on their own.

Simple figures though speak volumes.

In 1700 the population of the British Isles is around 5 million; by 1750 around 5.7 million; by 1800 the industrial revolution has led to an acceleration and it is speeding upwards at 7.8 million.

In 1700, the population of the colonies is perhaps 250,000; by 1750 it is 1.2 million; by 1800, it's 5.3 million. Note that perhaps one in five are of African descent.

In 1700, the biggest city is Boston with around 7,000 souls, followed by New York which has 5,000. By 1720, Boston has around 12,000, Philadelphia 10,000 and New York 7,000. By 1790, Philadelphia is the largest with 42,000, followed by New York (33,000) Boston (18,000) Charleston (16,000) and Baltimore (13,000).

What this should tell you is that America is a largely small town phenomenon, but one of many, many small towns.

At these rates, the United States will overtake the United Kingdom's population sometime in the middle of the nineteenth century. If Britain's chances of holding down such a large fractious population was impossible in the 1770s, how much more remarkable is it to fend off the growing giant in the War of 1812. Canada's population from Conquest to 1812 has risen from only 90,000 to 500,000 – a huge increase, partly down to Loyalist exiles, but it's still only a fraction of their southern neighbours. A fifth live in Upper Canada, a fifth in the Maritimes, and three fifths in Lower Canada with Montreal as the hub.

By contrast, London has a population of perhaps 600,000 in 1700, and 1.1 million in 1801. That leviathan is, however, an anomaly. The next biggest cities in 1700 (Bristol, Norwich or the like) are closer to the American size with perhaps 20-30,000 inhabitants and grow at a more aligned rate.

Trade

North America is not yet as rich as England, but it is swiftly catching up. It's also becoming an important export market. Have a look at these figures; in 1714, the total value of Britain's exports to

New England is £164,650 7s 6d; to New York £54,629 15s 5d; and Pennsylvania (or Pensilvania as it is officially written) £16,182 7s 7d. This gives some measure of their respective importance.

By contrast however, the sugar colonies draw in £407,233 7s 1d. African trade means exports worth £51,912 6s 2d, but even this is during a bad year and is normally 3 or 4 times that figure.

So you can see that at the start of the eighteenth century the Caribbean islands are far more important to the British economy than the continental mainland. No wonder European invasion fleets are so keen to head towards them, to damage trade and seize them as bargaining counters during peace talks.

But as the population grows and communities become more settled, wealthier and more needful, trade opportunities grow. The trade figures for the American colonies are up by a consistent quarter just a decade later, whereas the sugar colonies are seeing huge economic shifts meaning the figure drops by a quarter or goes up by a third.

The American colonies remain though hugely underdeveloped in terms of their industries, and overwhelmingly reliant on British capital for investment. By contrast, there is a huge export market for raw goods, and immense opportunities to clear virgin land to increase cultivation. Investment of local wealth has as a result gone into land clearance rather than in manufactures (making things). This has also incidentally led to those with some technical skills shifting into agriculture as planters once they make some money, since despite there being plenty of job prospects and good incomes available for skilled workers, such is the prestige that rather than being a tradesman working for someone else they prefer to be self-employed.

Due to taxes, themselves levied because these items are seen as luxuries, certain products cost more. These include soap, salt, candles, and leather.

Livestock doesn't tend to get exported, due to obvious shipping constraints. An exception in the 1720s is horses, which are transported in significant numbers from New England to Surinam and the French islands in return for sugar, molasses and rum. This obviously is unhelpful for Britain's own sugar islands as it means they lose a competitive advantage.

By the 1750s, around 96,000 hogsheads of tobacco are annually exported from Virginia and Maryland, exclusively via British bottoms (ie boats). Of this, around 14,000 service the British market; the rest is sold on the European market. Remarkably, European governments have banned growing it domestically since they find it far easier to tax it on arrival to collect the revenue, meaning that these two provinces enjoy something approaching a monopoly. Profitability is not, however, as high as sugar, which has the added end product generated from surplus that is rum.

Peculiarly, of foodstuffs, the Carolinas have discovered that rice is a more profitable crop than corn (wheat). While it is not a common local staple, it is seen as a potentially useful source of starch. Beware of investing in Georgian silk, as despite hopes it does not prove so productive. The dye known as indico is a safer bet, as is dealing in a number of goods protected by Parliament such as British-made ropes, sail cloth, manufactured leather, or even oak bark. By the same token, beware of changes in the law that may emerge during the Revolution, such as the lifting of bans on the production of tobacco in Ireland in 1779.

Trade from French Canada has long been heavily fur reliant. But note also that exports of Ginseng from Montreal to China have become very lucrative. The Jesuits in particular have emerged as middle men with the Indian suppliers. However, don't overinvest in this market as the skills in harvesting the roots are not known in these parts, leading to inferior quality and ultimately to a diminished interest.

Slavery

Initially, slavery includes Indians. But by the 1730s the slaves in question are almost universally of African extraction, and commonly known by the title of 'negroes', from the Latin word for 'black'. They started to be imported in bulk into the Americas once it became clear that indentured servants - contractually-bound Englishmen - were not a satisfactory solution to the agricultural manpower needs of the south (in part due to high mortality rates).

Some observers from Britain may find attitudes to slavery perplexing, particularly in a setting of such anxious campaigning for personal freedoms. Leading slave owner statesmen include Franklin, Hancock, Jefferson, Lee, Madison, and Washington (who

A slave trader in Africa purchases men from a local ruler. Millions of Africans have been shipped over the Atlantic and slaves now comprise a sizeable part of the population in some areas.

did however free many). Jefferson's first draft of the Declaration of Independence condemns the practise while blaming it on the British and accepting it as a reality. By contrast, Franklin, Hamilton and Jay (and by extension, a number of Federalists) are active supporters of their own state's anti-slavery campaigns. Jefferson's view differs in that unlike other southerners who are more attached to the model, he also envisages resettling the freed slaves in distinct colonies of their own, an idea that unhelpfully then gains a different traction in the emancipated north. He also notably proposes (but fails to get through) an element of the Virginia state constitution that would have meant no one could be born or brought into slavery after 1800, a compromise that would have thus changed things generationally.

The issue is highly polarised and you will already have an opinion on the subject. Let's step back for a moment and review matters. Slavery has been a part of the Americas for many years now – it's first legalised in 1641 in Massachusetts. It also carries an inherent risk. The slave uprising in the Carolinas in 1739 known as the Stono Rebellion for example triggers harsher treatment for slaves. Communities with large slave populations such as Virginia's have cells packed with ringleaders and supposed mutineers.

English Common Law has long been ambiguous on the legal force of slavery. There were many slaves in Anglo-Saxon England, though the Normans preferred a system that tied dependents to property under obligations rather than as possessions. Colonial possessions manned by slaves generated a new class of individuals that had largely been absent from English society since the feudal period.

The ambiguities come to a head as the eighteenth century approached. In 1690, a court ruled that a slave (Katherine Auker) expelled from an English home by an expat Barbados planter could not be banned from earning a living in his absence.

In the meantime, several colonies passed laws banning manumission. A legal review in England, the Yorke-Talbot Ruling of 1729, declares that a slave's arrival in England from the plantations did not change his condition, and he might be compelled to return.

This might have been challenged in 1757, except that the slave died before the case was judged. From 1762 though, other judges start to adjudge that slavery is innately contrary to domestic English law.

In the event, Yorke-Talbot is overturned in 1772 in the James Sommersett case, which adjudges that a slave cannot be send abroad purely for running away. The eloquence of the counsel acting for Mr. Sommersett is celebrated. After pointing to the iniquities of a Jamaican legal practice that allows children to become what amounted to war booty, he expands,

"For the air of England; I think, however, it has been gradually purifying ever since the reign of Elizabeth. Mr. Dunning seems to have discovered so much, as he finds it changes a slave into a servant; though unhappily he does not think it of efficacy enough to prevent that pestilent disease reviving, the instant the poor man is obliged to quit (voluntarily quits, and legally it seems we ought to say,) this happy country. However, it has been asserted, and is now repeated by me, this air is too pure for a slave to breathe in: I trust, I shall not quit this court without certain conviction of the truth of that assertion."

It does not quite turn out that way. Strictly speaking, the new ruling does not change the status of the 15,000 slaves estimated present at that time in England, still considering them as goods and chattel even if converted to the Christian faith. Indeed in 1785 the same judge, Lord Mansfield, later also rules that slaves do not have to be paid for their labour despite himself here calling the practice "odious" and a relic. But the Sommersett ruling does prevent their removal by force, and it keeps their actual legal status in England open to review.

Meanwhile the matter is evolving with a peculiar twist in Scotland. The John Wedderburn case of 1778 resolves that in that legal jurisdiction it is unlawful to employ a man without pay, therefore slavery is illegal. But bonded labour does meanwhile remain legal for those native Scotsmen forced to dig mines or grow crops for small sums.

In the colonies there is also a shift taking place, at least in the north. In 1774, Rhode Island and Connecticut ban slave imports from overseas. At the same time though, Rhode Island maintains a slave market, and both have laws that discriminate.

In 1777, Vermont officially bans slavery. It also provides for votes for "free negroes". Slavery is subsequently banned (in some cases, phased out) by the state constitutions of Pennsylvania (1780), Massachusetts and New Hampshire (1783), Connecticut and Rhode Island (1784), New York (1799) and New Jersey (1804). Crucially, the Northwest Ordinance of 1787 stipulates that the old 'Ohio territories' are to be non-slave lands.

By independence, there are approaching half a million slaves in America. This reality is both admitted and suppressed by the constitution, which in assigning weight to the various states counts slaves (the word is not even admitted by name) as three fifths of a free man. This also commits those states to pay that fraction as a share of the federal taxes too, so it comes at a cost.

In 1791, the bitter events around the Haiti Revolt generate a backlash against relaxing slavery laws. Even so, noted anti-slavery campaigner William Wilberforce in Britain is able in 1792 to pass a bill that calls for a gradual abolition of the trade. It is a small, perhaps disappointing yet important step, knocked back though by more pressing concerns for both Parliament and the Admiralty when war escalates with France.

Meanwhile, Congress has been grappling with what to do with runaway slaves, since the Constitution establishes an obligation to hand them back. It is not resolved to anyone's satisfaction and kidnapping remains a typical response.

In 1807, Britain's Parliament passes the law that abolishes the slave trade as far as the British Empire is concerned. A small fleet is posted off the African coast (at significant cost in terms of finances and sailors' lives given the climate, it should be noted). Currently the remit of these ships is limited only to those countries that have also banned the slave trade - hopefully over time this number will grow and they will have greater effect. Because slavery is still widespread in the Americas, including British plantations in the Caribbean but especially in the southern states and in Brazil, there is a big market. For now, false flag smuggling and use of vessels under Latin American papers allows for huge legal loopholes. Congress bans foreign slave imports in 1808, but one senses it will be some years yet before it accepts the Royal Navy boarding American ships to effectively track down these smugglers of death. It also means that slave society in America itself will change and 'Americanise', losing its disparate African roots over time.

So, if you are travelling in America, be aware of rather different views on this matter. A number of British institutions may be shareholders in plantations, and conditions can vary significantly, but seeing the actual sites may bring some uncomfortable distant realities home.

Money

Currency

Colonial money takes a familiar form - Pounds, Shillings and Pence; £/L, s, and d. However, these are colony pounds and are worth less than a British one, though the exact value varies from colony to colony. The actual bullion coins are often of Spanish origin, which is why you may hear talk of dollars.

The Spanish dollar coin is acceptable in many areas as the weight and quality of its silver content is widely trusted. Some think the dollar will become the currency of North

As a gentleman and a traveller you will be familiar with the concept of paper money. It is the means by which individuals or small groups can issue a pledge of repayment of a sum, and for the note itself to be traded as a redeemable figure. The greatest and most secure issuer is the English state.

You will be delighted to learn that your Bank of England notes are held in the highest esteem, though you should be highly cautious if taking other forms of credit or promissory papers with you. Note also that each colony issues its own forms of paper currency, whose values vary considerably. Forget the old five and ten shilling notes that used to be issued in Scotland, and think more in terms of some of the paper promissory notes being handed around in Yorkshire. Paper has a much bigger role on his side of the Atlantic, and for much smaller sums - certainly for sums as small as a shilling.

Paper is hugely important in the colonies. Gold and silver is starting to make something of an appearance as some of the paper notes start to be suppressed, and banned by Parliament completely in 1772.

Of course, notes carry the guarantee of repayment in gold by the issuer to the last holder. But one pernicious aspect, and something which strengthens trust in English notes, has been the move to add a wretched clause to colony-issued notes that allows the local government the right to delay such payment by several years. The problem is, these particular notes do not have interest attached to them, which means that the person would be missing out of several years' worth of interest had he invested the sum somewhere else instead. So be careful when you accept notes of high value to see whether or not you are in fact exchanging good English notes for bad colony ones that you can't get rid of - or even worse, that you unwittingly accept a bad exchange rate.

In 1722 Pennsylvania passes a law that puts their notes on equal footing with their face value in gold or silver, but that doesn't oblige you to accept such a note valued at a rate that nobody still actually believes. In some colonies, one hundred pounds sterling is considered as worth one hundred and thirty pounds local; in the worst cases it has been valued at eleven hundred. It's all because the local traders realise that paper notes are being printed in numbers that are utterly disproportionate to what the taxes actually bring in, at terms of redemption that question the end value if not the actual probability of getting your original money back at all.

So the British Government has decided to step in. Here we might quote the eminently sensible Adam Smith; "No law, therefore, could be more equitable than the act of parliament, so unjustly complained of in the colonies, which declared that no paper currency to be emitted there in time coming should be a legal tender of payment."

Pennsylvania also tried to arbitrarily drop the exchange rate of silver and gold coins, so that coins were in face value terms worth more locally. At first sight this was a clever way of ensuring that precious metal was kept in the colony. However, it was soon found that the price of imports rose to match, meaning just as much gold and silver was exported in coinage as before. So you need to be aware that even the coins in your purse may not be valued at their face value.

A peculiar alternative is effectively a form of barter. "Tobacco notes" are essentially certificates relating to quality controlled stocks of that produce. As they are redeemable and easily carried, they make good promissory notes for much of the century.

After 1775, Continental Currency begins to circulate in areas under rebel control. This is paper money that gets overprinted. Hold on to these for any length of time and you will lose money, as the real value goes down cataclysmically. It doesn't help that the British are putting into circulation considerable amounts of effective forgeries as well, even advertising their wares to hand out to people travelling into rebel areas! It's an ingenious strategy.

The experience leads to central government alone being given the right to issue paper money that isn't immediately redeemable, which in effect means establishing a common currency by the back door. Moreover, since gold and silver coin values are universal depending on their purity, this is bolstered by the establishment of a U.S. Mint in 1792, creating a common set of coins of uniform value. The idea of having 100 cents to a dollar though is just too revolutionary to catch on.

Spanish currency remains too widespread to be replaced entirely, so if you are thinking of stopping off in Florida as well during your stay you might consider simplifying matters and carrying Spanish silver.

Canada's currency generates even more confusion after conquest. Paper money issued in Québec under the old regime was banned in 1759, so don't accept those notes. Montreal initially accepts the New York system at around 1.78 to the London Pound, but by 1764 changes to the Halifax system which simplifies matters in Canada. Quebec sticks with its own Pound at around 1.33 to the Pound, until following Halifax in 1777. New York money circulates in parallel, but then the trade routes to the rebellious colonies close. So for Canada after the American Revolution the base currency is that of Halifax running at roughly 1.10 to the Pound. Newfoundland sticks with its own, valued at around 1.15. However, add to that mix the official use of English Pounds when dealing with London, and a different currency called Army Sterling to cater for the multiplicity of postings a soldier might get.

So the long and the short of it is to remember to ask which Pound you are being quoted a price in!

Banking

A silver sixpence of King George III. Despite the political turmoil, you will find these coins are readily taken by merchants.

Banks have also begun to appear on this side of the Atlantic. These issue paper money secured on property of borrowers. An example is the Pennsylvania Land Bank, supported by Mr Franklin. As we have earlier noted, later banks begin to issue excessive notes and on bad terms, contrary to English laws set in place after the South Sea Bubble collapse, so do be careful when changing your money.

The War of 1812 leads to banks once again reverting to type, literally. The US had a central bank, but this was run down in 1811, largely due to fears of British influence. But removing it kills a safeguard. Too many notes are issued, and inflation hits again. This leads to considerable distrust of the wisdom of developing a federal central bank. It seems that bank notes with all their controversies are not after all going to play a central part in the future currency make up of the United States.

Weights and Measures

The British Imperial Troy Pound was regulated in 1758. Yards, gallons and bushels have equally been set out by Parliament. It is possible of course that future regulations, either in America or London, may yet lead to divergence as measuring technologies advance. But for now they will largely be familiar.

Information Technology

Communications

As back home, the town crier provides a useful medium for learning the latest official news.

The Media

Newspapers are beginning to become an important feature of colonial life. In 1729, Benjamin Franklin takes over the newly-launched Pennsylvania Gazette, which in time becomes the best selling newspaper. It's also the first to publish political cartoons; Franklin's dismembered snake with the caption "join or die" (representing the disjointed colonies) starting the trend. The paper will attract some of the most important essayists and polemicists, and Franklin notably defends his publishing a wide range of views by pointing out the opinions of men are as various as their faces.

You might also try out a copy of the Boston News-Letter (from 1704 til the Revolution) or Boston Gazette, New York's Weekly Journal, and in Williamsburg the Virginia Gazette. News tends to be a mixture of the parochial and what's been gleaned from arriving vessels.

As politics heats up you will find an array of propaganda sheets being handed around. These herald the explosion of the newspaper trade, which are often party aligned. There is an attempt by the Federalists to muzzle this new free press as part of the Alien and Sedition Acts in 1798, by restricting the rights of editors to criticise the executive, but as the French crisis passed and the Federalists lost power these laws are allowed to fall.

Learning

The first colonial library was founded in Philadelphia in 1731, again by Mr Franklin. He also in 1750 plays a role in the establishment of the Academy of Philadelphia, which significantly shifts the emphasis of the syllabus away from educating members of the clergy.

Not all American erudition stems from this one man, though! Harvard College was set up in 1636 by the government of Massachusetts Bay. It's named after an early benefactor who provided a large legacy of land and books. John Adams is a later graduate, along with seven other signers of the Declaration of Independence.

The College of William and Mary was established in 1693. It would have been set up in 1618, but plans were ruined by an Indian war. Both Washington and Jefferson study here. It's also home to the first fraternity (Phi Beta Kappa in 1776 - students take it shortly afterwards toHarvard and Yale). It is the only American college to have its own coat of arms.

Yale in Connecticut dates from 1701, though only becoming a college in 1718. The College of New Jersey (1746) was moved to Princeton after ten years: Nassau Hall is where a handful of cornered redcoats surrender after an engagement in 1777. King's College in New York is renamed Columbia after the Revolution. Rhode Island College includes amongst its early backers several members of the Brown family. Queen's College is in New Jersey, and New Hampshire has Dartmouth College. As colleges tend to reflect the religious ideals of their founders, in 1789 a Catholic teaching establishment is also founded at Georgetown with strong Jesuit influence. Of course, the creation of many other institutions looks set to follow - but only for gentlemen of substance.

Law and Disorder

Crime

A surfeit of opportunity has not caused the extinction of criminality. Be on your guard as you would on any European trip.

Crown Rights

Do not vandalise property carrying the government sign, that is to say an upwards pointing arrowhead. This is particularly true with respect to chopping down those large white pines that are so marked, as these are admiralty trees, reserved in order to make masts for warships. From 1722 you need a license to cut those wider than a foot, at risk of a fine. This starts to get properly enforced in the 1760s, when settlers also have to pay for the privilege of having their land surveyed. From 1771 there's also a premium on white oak staves. Timber management acts as one of the local grievances, and indeed triggers an ugly incident called the Pine Tree Riot.

Policing

In rural areas, you will find a sheriff appointed by the governor. A number of towns use the Watch system. In the cities from the middle of the century, the Watch changes from a sort of militia duty to become a paid post. This is a far from uniform process so do not necessarily expect those supposedly keeping the peace to involve themselves over enthusiastically in any brutal fight. They may be unwilling volunteers.

Remember that as in England, there is a bewildering variety of law courts, just as there are different law codes covering different aspects of society. Hence you will find in operation common law, statute law, maritime law, ecclesiastical law, the law of corporations, and local law and customs. In particular with respect to the latter, reflect on how puritanical the particular colony has historically been and you'll have a heads up on how you'll be treated if you've gone a little over the top on the gin. You might also be usefully cognisant that various colonies apply their own variations of the legal system. New Jersey uses juries more than New York does. Pennsylvania and Delaware have no Court of Chancery or Probates. Georgia only has common law courts, and appeals go from one jury to another. The four eastern colonies peculiarly develop an automatic appeals system to produce the 'best of three' jury results. All this shouldn't concern you unduly unless you are a practising lawyer, however.

Self Defence

With all this in mind, gentlemen should be aware of the law pertaining to their rights to defend themselves. They should already largely be familiar with it.

Murder se defendendo is where one man kills another when a quarrel breaks out and he has to do so to save his own life. This is called excusable homicide. Justifiable homicide is what happens when defending one's person, goods or house that takes place on the highway or indoors. Homicide is also permitted in support of a constable or officer of justice.

Under English law there is no provocation without a blow. If there is a blow that is returned by accidental excessive force, that is manslaughter. If someone is undertaking an illegal act such as shooting another man's chickens and the shot goes wild, then that is murder. An immediate response to provocation is manslaughter, but when undertaken after an interval it is murder.

Manslaughter is an invention that will baffle Scottish travellers but actually comes from the Benefit of Clergy. This is the surviving rag ends of the mediaeval legal system that the Church ran for its own members. The Church claimed as a privilege for its own members an exemption from the murder laws thanks to Deuteronomy Chapter 19, introducing a lesser charge that Queen Anne in turn subsequently extends across the whole community. The result is that if manslaughter happens thanks to a sudden fight or quarrel ("chance medley") the default is that the perpetrator forfeits his property, but can then bring a law case to get them back and sue for pardon; in a case of justifiable homicide you should instead plead not guilty to escape punishment.

By the eighteenth century, Benefit of Clergy is largely redundant. Famously it is resorted to after the so-called 'Boston Massacre' following the guilty verdicts against two of the soldiers involved. This means that the death penalty is avoided. The provision historically is that the condemned man can read the first verse of Psalm 51, though even this requirement was abolished in 1705 (usefully so as one of the soldiers could not read, so he would have had to memorise it). The punishment actually inflicted was being branded on the thumb with an 'M' so as to avoid being able to claim that defence again. In this instance, the somewhat antiquated legal solution proves politically convenient for all parties concerned.

51 Have mercy upon me, O God, according to thy loving kindness: according unto the multitude of thy tender mercies blot out my transgressions.

The opening verse from Deuteronomy 51, taken from the King James Bible. If you have to memorise the text due to reading issues, make sure you confirm how many lines you need to know - and pick the right bible version.

Punishment

Those found guilty will, of course, be punished accordingly. These are often spectator events in their own right, just as back home, since the best way to educate people of the perils of law breaking and to reassure the victims is to get everyone involved as witnesses. Punishments as you will be aware vary, from mock executions to make a point; disfigurement such as slicing the ear; spells in prison (this costs money, so largely for debtors until they pay up); time in the pillory; lashes; being tied astride an uncomfortable wooden horse; and of course hanging.

Mob justice is an occupational risk for agents of the Crown that even pistols increasingly fail to deter.

Prisoners of War

Considering that rebels are, confirmed by 1776 Act of Parliament, participating in the crimes of High Treason or of Piracy, the rebellion is dealt with rather generously in the circumstances.

Life as a prisoner of war is not amusing, particularly if you are not an officer, have no social standing and innate sense of honour, and are thus not in a position to offer parole. Owing to General Washington's reluctance to exchange his own men for veteran redcoats, prisoner exchanges are soon halted. Since every large building available has already been turned into a prison by the British, including churches and factories, it means that large numbers of continentals held have to be bundled onto hulks.

This is no different a process from how prisoners are dealt with over in Europe, but proves even more unhealthy in these waters. One vessel, HMS Jersey, gains a particular reputation as a death ship, perhaps as a consequence of being the one most written about.

It's originally a warship, then a troop ship, adapted into storage ship, then a hospital ship. But after prisoners set fire to two other prison ships, it gets converted once again.

Conditions are grim, and many prisoners die from smallpox, poor food, and inherently dismal surroundings. Those suffering from war wounds are particularly susceptible. But then, what should rebels of any country expect in this day and age? Consider what happened only a generation ago in Britain itself after the last Jacobite uprising, or what has happened in Poland after its recent revolt.

Both sides hold prisoners of war. The Saratoga Convention allowed for British soldiers to return to Britain under a pledge of avoiding further engagement in the war. This would have meant removing redcoats in exchange for more numerous American sailors, which the British largely did not want to do. The agreements fall and this leaves the Americans with a "Convention Army" of prisoners of its own to have to deal with. It further provides a motive for better treatment of rebels in British hands. It is nevertheless clear that their conditions are hardly model and you would be advised to avoid becoming a prisoner of either side during this conflict.

No Quarter

There is a lot of black propaganda going on about atrocities. For instance, take the vilified Lt Col Tarleton. The surrender terms he offers his opponent at Wacsaws in 1780 (which were turned down) allow the militia to go home under parole; officers to take with them their private baggage, horses and side arms; and just the Continental (ie the rebel central army) soldiers to go to a nearby garrison where even then they receive the same provisions as British soldiers.

But some fighting during the Revolution indeed becomes very bitter. This is particularly the case in the South where locals are fighting each other in higher proportion. Gentlemanly standards can slip, especially in the middle of a fight and as casualties mount. If you hear the cry of "No Quarter", you are advised not to attempt to surrender unless to a very senior officer visibly attempting to halt the process.

> "Antiquity affords us no eclaircisement respecting the future government of America. I see no reason to doubt, that Great Britain, may not long retain us in constitutional obedience. Time, the destroyer of human affairs, may indeed, end her political life by a gentle decay. Like Rome, she may be constrained to defend herself from the Huns, and Alaricks of the North. Ingratefully should we endeavour to precipitate her political demise, she will devise every expedient to retain our obedience; and rather than fail, will participate those provinces amongst the potent states of Europe."
>
> James Chalmers, Loyalist pamphleteer, 1776

Chapter 4

Culture and Social Mores

Religion

The Established Church

The Church of England is the established church back home. The situation here, however, is more complex given the different religious groups that founded the various colonies. As of 1706, for instance, it is named the official church of South Carolina, and is the designated official faith of half the colonies, all towards the south. Here, taxes are raised to support the priests.

As a consequence of close association between this church and the government (priests swear an oath of allegiance to the monarch), you will find it in a greatly weakened state by the Low Season as many clergy have to flee patriot death threats and are not even in a position to safely mount the pulpit. It also means that they don't write the history books, and get tarnished by competing clergy as a result.

Church government is highly decentralised and reliant upon local prominent members of the parish, who play a leading part in the church courts that govern court cases on moral issues such as missing services or adultery.

One benefit the Revolution does bring though is the establishment of a genuinely American church. Previously, it was part of the see of the Bishop of London. Politically that is now inexpedient. But how does one continue the apostolic tradition (the succession of priests since the time of Christ) while avoiding any implications of treasonable activity by having to take that oath? The first American bishop travels to Scotland where he is consecrated by Anglican bishops who don't need to swear allegiance there.

Other Churches

Dissenting churches are very strong in some areas, and as of 1689 have been officially tolerated by London. In Anglican colonies, authorising licenses can come at the cost of still having to pay the church tax though and preventing members from standing for election.

These various churches are far from united, however, and there is something of a back history of some colonies oppressing even other protestant groups, forcing them to leave to set up dissenting colonies of their own.

These days things are a bit more tolerant in that regard. A curious development though happens in 1734. The Great Awakening is a religious revival movement that starts off in Massachusetts and lasts for a decade, spreading widely. It's a time of engaging sermons and missionary zeal. As a visitor you will find it either invigorating or tiresome.

From 1772, foreign protestants settling in America, or serving there in the Engineers or Royal American Regiment, are granted British nationality.

Is the Pope Catholic?

If you thought some protestant groups had it bad, you've not seen how the more zealous colonies deal with the Catholics. As at 1700 both Massachusetts and New York have banned the presence of Roman Catholic priests, on potential pain of death. Mind you, to be fair the Pope is taking sides with the royal succession and backing the (Catholic) Stuart pretenders, so politics is part of it.

Maryland was set up as a Catholic colony, but by 1700 while there are Catholics resident, the Glorious Revolution means that the tables have turned. Test oaths mean that like in England they can't take office; they are banned from some jobs; and from 1718 they lose their voting rights. Georgia's statutes from as recently as 1732 allow religious freedom for all settlers except specifically Catholics.

If you want to see a Catholic church, for a while there simply isn't one. The colonies get their first in 1732, in Philadelphia. But even by the time of the Revolution there is only a score of priests to cater for the few thousand believers. As you might expect, since there is no Anglican bishop specially for the English-speaking colonies, there is no Catholic bishop either.

By contrast, after the Conquest, Catholicism is given a privileged position in Quebec to ensure its loyalty or at least neutrality. It works. So if you want to chat about doctrinal difficulties with a Roman bishop, or need last rites, hang on til you get to here.

Minority religions

It is vaguely conceivable you may bump into rarer faiths brought by seafarers. We can't advise you on this point as our knowledge of the East India trade and Hindou sailors is limited.

Another possibility though is the Jewish religion. In 1700, there are perhaps 200-300 believers in the colonies, though they face restrictions in some colonies and an enduring struggle to be recognised as local citizens. The first synagogue is built in 1730. By the end of the century, there are perhaps 2,500-3,000 Jews in the United States.

Deists

This controversial European fad has crossed the Atlantic. As you are aware, it expresses a general belief in a divine entity without going into too much of the detail, especially on the process of worship. This has the advantage of crossing denominational and even religious boundaries, at the cost of good order and common sense. Some of the most prominent rebel leaders are said to be Deists. Others are not but are instead secularists. Both are reasons for a gentleman to take caution at the dinner table.

Freemasons

A number of lodges are being established in the colonies. Visitors with Freemasonry connections on extended stays will find a number of eminent figures participating in meetings they might attend. One analysis suggests that there may be a hundred lodges by the Middle Season, which makes the organisation an unusual common element across the colonies. Some suggest Franklin's Albany Plan for a mild common government for the colonies is suspiciously analogous to the way the lodges are organised.

Personal connections made in these meetings might conceivably prove useful either in business terms (especially where credit is concerned), or in times of strife given the presence of so many future rebel leaders. But lodge members will know better than this author.

By contrast, the Irish Loyalist organisation known as the Orange Order is introduced through the military. Its first lodge is introduced to New Brunswick via the garrison in 1783. Officers posted to North America after this time may find this a useful networking tool.

Embassies and Consulates

The colonies are part of the British Empire, and so national embassies are sited at the Court of St James in London. Enquiries should be directed through these in the first instance.

Travellers with Disabilities

You are recommended to bring prosthetics with you, as locally-manufactured items will be rudimentary. After 1800, visit Mr Potts of London for articulated legs.

Wildlife

America is a dangerous place. Wolves, bears, moose, venomous snakes, mountain lions, huge eagles, sharks and other creatures need to be fended off by more than a walking stick. Carry a rifle and travel noisily, unless there are also Indians around in which case carry a rifle and travel nervously.

Beware also of all manner of parlous bugs, especially spiders that in these parts can be fatal. You may need to delouse after crossing the Atlantic. Biting midges remind one of Scotland at its worst.

Some wildlife can turn you a profit. The best beaver pelts are those that have actually been worn against the skin for a year or more, to soften them up and remove the coarser hairs. The trading rate of one such pelt is a blanket, a pair of shoes, or a quarter of a pistol. Raccoon is common. Skins from wild cats, muskrats, otters, martens, and foxes (amongst others) bring in variable rates. Feathers can also be traded.

Monsters

This is the Enlightenment. There are no monsters.

Culture

Music

Music travels as readily as the sheet of paper upon which it is written. Thus you should encounter the sounds of all the great composers of our era. As you are already aware, examples include Vivaldi (d. 1741), Bach (d. 1750), Handel (d. 1759), Mozart (1756-1791), Haydn (1732-1809), and Beethoven (b.1770).

title in a lengthy bout in 1811. His trainer is another famous sparrer, another ex slave called Bill Richmond whom a British general had talent-spotted winning a brawl against several of his soldiers, and brought over to England to learn carpentry and pass on his sidestepping talents.

Outdoor pursuits

The scenery lends itself to watercolours for those with the skills. Those without them can shoot and stuff what they see instead. Try to do better than the King of Sweden has done with his dead lion, which (as the taxidermist has never seen a live one) looks like it has just taken a suppository.

Languages & Manners

The common language of the colonies is English. You should be aware, however, that languages spoken in European settlements taken over by the British Crown continue to exist. The French speakers of Acadia and Quebec we have in particular earlier referenced.

The Swedes and Finns that were subsumed into the Dutch colony leave the slightest of footprints: strangely, you'll probably find more of a Finnish imprint being made on Alaska after their home province in Europe is conquered by Russia.

You will find more of an opportunity to practise your German. The Georges as well as being king of the United Kingdom as you will recall are also the Prince Electors of Hanover, by which we basically mean the territories of most of Brunswick-Luneburg plus various bits subsequently bolted on. The personal connection, plus the protestant flavour of the colonies, encourages a number of Germans from Lutheran and Reformed churches to emigrate, especially to Pennsylvania, paying off their passage by fixed labour for several years on arrival. In addition, there are German-speaking Swiss, and exiled protestants from Austria. By 1790, there are an estimated 100,000 German speakers - in Maryland they make up one in eight of the population, and in Pennsylvania one in three (whence the 'Pennsylvania Deutsch', pronounced 'Dutch'). Perhaps 5,000 Hessians hired to fight on

Britain's behalf themselves decide to stay after losing the fight - largely, understandably, in these German-speaking areas.

Literacy in the more settled areas is very high. Expect nine men in ten, and one women in two, to be able to read by the middle of the century. The proportion is higher amongst property owners, and higher still in New England owing to a greater number of schools and a desire to encourage everyone to be able to read the bible. Slaves are not forbidden to be taught how to read, and

indeed some owners see it as a Christian duty, or as a way of increasing their worth; but others are very cautious about letting them write.

Manners

A gentleman will be aware of what good manners are expected of him. For those who have been a while in uncouth company, here are some established tips;

* Keep your hands in public display. Don't tap or drum or hum, or bite your nails.

* Don't spit into a fire.

* Avoid shaking your head, whispering, raising an eyebrow, a frothy mouth, or rolling your eyes.

* Don't point or stand too close when conversing.

* Do take off your hat and bow when meeting a person of substance.

* Don't remove any lice or fleas in public.

* Never show you are happy at a criminal's punishment. Avoid showing happiness in the company of ill people.

* Stand up if someone of whatever rank comes up to talk to you; offer seats according to their status.

* Give way when passing people of superior status. If accompanying someone, the social superior stands on the right.

* Walk in a measured way without running, dawdling, or waving your arms around.

* Don't blame a man for failing if he attempts something well.

* Don't speak a foreign language if not everyone can understand.

* Avoid spreading gossip.
* If someone of substance comes into a conversation half way through it, repeat what's been said for his benefit.
* If in the company of your social betters, keep quiet until asked to comment, then straighten your back, take your hat off and answer succinctly.
* When eating, don't gobble the food down. Avoid showing how much you like the food. Don't lean on the table (a hand can rest there, though). Cut the bread with a clean knife. You can dunk your bread in sauce, but don't stuff it all in your mouth at the same time and don't blow on your food.
* Don't show anger at table.
* It is impolite to eat the meat once cut with the knife still in your hand: just use the fork.

Social Class

There are very few peers of the realm in the colonies. While technically an early Jamestown Indian ally becomes Lord of the Manor, this is not a full peerage. Nor is a baronet, and while scores upon scores of baronetcies of Nova Scotia were sold by the early Stuarts to pay for its colonisation, the owners stayed at home.

As a measure of their rarety, we can only think of three peers who end up buried in these parts. There's the third Viscount Howe (dies fighting the French, brother of the two Howes in charge of the army and navy during the Revolutionary War); Lord Maryland (last royal governor there, made a Maryland baronet in exile, well respected, dies after the Revolution while trying to sort out some family land rights); and Lord Fairfax, who lives on his Virginia estates before they get confiscated by revolutionaries.

That makes establishing order of precedence at dinner parties a little easier. Concentrate on distinguishing between gentry, artisans, labourers and slaves.

Chapter 5

The Revolution at a Glance

Finishing off your breakfast while waiting for the regiment to get into battle order? You may find the following a useful speedy guide to determine whether you should pocket your valuables before joining the line, in anticipation of a hasty retreat afterwards. This isn't a complete list of course, and excludes many smaller skirmishes, a number of which we explore in the timeline at the end of this tome. You'll note the British have a greater tendency of winning the major engagements, though it's more difficult to tell if on aggregate the smaller ones that aren't listed count more.

In any case, victories too often come at a major cost in casualties that simply can't be replaced; surrendered forces add to these difficulties; and nobody is quite able to mobilise what is quite often very significant (but very intimidated) Loyalist support. In a war of morale, the rebels also seem to get the lucky breaks.

At first it's a struggle to keep the Revolution going. Then it becomes a fight about how total are the terms, and Saratoga opens up the possibility of total independence. Foreign support means that British resources are fatally distracted in a global life-or-death struggle against an overwhelming coalition. From then on, what actually counts is trying to hold onto what the colonial commanders can, and by aiming to strike a blow at the heart of the rebel forces in Virginia, Cornwallis in effect surrenders the Deep South (and, at a pinch, any hope of clinging onto a New York enclave too).

Pick your battles carefully in this. Artillery does not discriminate.

Battle	Name and Date of the Battle	Result and Consequences
Lexington	19 April 1775	British force moves to confiscate militia arms. Stand off at Lexington Green. First British volley may have had no balls loaded. The second does. Militia scatter. British able to continue on to Concord.
Concord	19 April 1775	British attempt to seize arms only marginally successful. Another stand off escalates. Engaged British troops withdraw, then reinforced and push back minutemen. British march back to Boston but take significant casualties in process. British initial tactical victory, strategic defeat.
Bunker (properly speaking, Breed's) Hill	16 June1775	Boston militias pre-empt British moves to secure outskirts of the city. Pyrrhic victory as repeated assaults take the rebel positions, but at significant cost.
Quebec	31 December 1775	Rebels invade Canada in September, taking Montreal. They advance onto Quebec city. Attacking during a snow storm, one wing is halted as its commander is killed; the other pushes on but is trapped. The rebels resort to a siege, which fails. Canada is saved.
Trois Rivières	8 June 1776	Americans advancing into Canada are guided into a swamp. Extricating themselves they encounter British units, which break them. The rebels are rolled back out of Canada
Sullivan's Island	28 June 1776	British launch an expedition against Charleston. Scanty interposing field defences resist their naval bombardment and the attackers withdraw to New York.
Long Island (Brooklyn Heights)	27 August 1776	British forces land and enfilade the rebels. The rearguard is annihilated. Washington manages to withdraw across to Manhattan overnight, thereby saving his army.
Harlem Heights	16 September 1776	British push against withdrawing continental forces almost leads to one unit being outflanked. British units pull back. Marginal Continental victory restores some morale, but withdrawal continues.

White Plains	28 October 1776	Washington's gradual strategic withdrawal continues. Howe attempts to intercept. Washington is pushed from his defensive positions and the British pursuit continues.
Fort Washington	16 November 1776	Continental Army garrison remaining on Long Island does not vacate its position. It is subsequently stormed and 3,000 prisoners taken. Rebel morale sinks lower.
Trenton	26 December 1776	Making use of the cover of the inclement weather, as well as the cover provided by Christmas (the cad), Washington crosses the Delaware and assaults the unsuspecting (though note, not inebriated) Hessian garrison at Trenton. 1,000 prisoners taken, Continental morale restored.
Princeton	3 January 1777	After Trenton, manoeuvres follow. Washington holds off the British at Assunpink near Trenton on 2 January. But he marches on Princeton overnight and overruns that small garrison too. The Continental Army's successes are sufficient to ensure it will survive into the new year.
Oriskany	6 August 1777	During the advance on Saratoga, British units besiege Fort Stanwix. A relief column is ambushed by Loyalists and Iroquois and defeated.
Bennington	16 August 1777	A British foraging party is ambushed by a much larger force and destroyed. Burgoyne's position now becomes difficult as Indian support diminishes as do supplies.
Brandywine Creek	11 September 1777	Howe leads an advance on Philadelphia. Strategically this means not supporting Burgoyne at Saratoga. But he encounters Washington at the Brandywine in the largest land battle so far, and defeats him. Howe seizes Philadelphia. Washington though is able to escape with his forces intact.
Freeman's Farm	19 September 1777	First Battle of Saratoga. Burgoyne pushes on rebel positions. Arnold's dispositions prevent a US rout and create significant British casualties.
Germantown	4 October 1777	Washington advances on a large British garrison near Philadelphia. Some initial success ends in chaos in the fog. Rebels defeated, Howe's army intact.

Saratoga	7 October 1777	Burgoyne by now is heavily outnumbered at Saratoga. He tests the rebel positions, but the reconnoitring unit is overwhelmed, which precipitates a broader defeat. The rebel army is now seen to be a capable adversary. Burgoyne is forced to surrender. French pre-empt the possibility of an early settled peace by declaring war on Britain.
Monmouth	28 June 1778	British withdrawal from Philadelphia is interrupted by a Continental attack. The Continentals are repelled and the British march resumes.
Waxhaws	29 May 1780	Small cavalry force under Tarleton overwhelms a small force of Continentals. Surrender not immediately accepted. Environment of atrocities grows.
Camden	16 August 1780	British capture Charleston. Forces engage each other at the strategic junction of Camden. US militia panics and flees swiftly. Continental forces then routed by Cornwallis, despite having a smaller army. Pendulum in Carolinas swings to British.
King's Mountain	7 October 1780	Surprise rebel attack destroys Loyalist militia. Loyalists in Carolinas cowed. Cornwallis resolves to move the war north.
Cowpens	17 January 1781	Two small forces engage with utterly disproportionate results. Tarleton's attack, as anticipated, pushes rebels back but into stronger positions. His unit is destroyed. Loyalist morale in the south breaks.
Guilford Courthouse	15 March 1781	Cornwallis encounters an army twice the size of his own in North Carolina. He assaults it and it routs, but at major cost. The rebel force remains intact and a local threat, thus able to secure the south against Loyalists once Cornwallis has gone.
Hobkirk's Hill	25 April 1781	Second Battle of Camden. Small scale engagement in which rebel push is driven off.

Green Spring	6 July 1781	Cornwallis is running rampant across Virginia. He deceives Lafayette into believing his forces have mostly crossed the James River. The Continental Army attacks what it thinks is just a rearguard. Only a mad assault buys time for its exposed units to withdraw.
The Capes	5 September 1781	The Royal Navy has had a good war so far. However, a fleet to fleet action against a larger French force ends in a withdrawal, meaning local French control continues. The French are thus able to reinforce their besieging forces at Yorktown, and the British army is trapped.
Eutaw Springs	8 September 1781	Continental forces have exploited Cornwallis's absence to roll up the southern colonies. The Charleston garrison marches out. A foraging unit is ambushed. In the main engagement, the British break through two lines but are halted by the third, break, and retreat back to the camp under pursuit. A unit in a building then causes the pursuing rebels to break. Notional British victory but south largely still remains in rebel hands which is important for the peace negotiations.
Yorktown	9 September 1781	Washington deceives British forces into believing an attack on New York is imminent, but instead reinforces Continental forces in Virginia. Cornwallis is penned in and a siege commences. Reinforcements arrive too late. He surrenders. The Government in London teeters and falls. Peace negotiations begin.

American general George Washington issues orders to his officers at the Battle of Yorktown.

Serving with Your Regiment

It may be that you are in the colonies as you are attached to your regiment, which has either been despatched for war or for garrison duties. In such circumstances it will already be made plain to you what standards you are expected to maintain. Those with experience fighting in continental Europe may take some adjusting, both to the general lack of cavalry in this theatre but also the underhand tactics of colonial units of whatever origin. The locals have an alarming tendency to go to ground, fire unsportingly from cover, reload lying down, and aim specifically at officers.

Artillery is another arm that is encountered less frequently, particularly when they have to be dragged through wild woods. When it appears it is a game changer. Sieges near rivers lend themselves to sailors dragging ship cannons to your aid in such circumstances. Engineers are more commonplace, and often supplied from locals.

Note that for periods of conflict, you will likely encounter a variety of units of militia. These are widely held in contempt by regular soldiers, since though they can have local knowledge, they are far more likely to run away, especially when faced with volley fire followed by a bayonet charge. Some units do play a credible part in certain campaigns, for instance the colonial regiments forming up for the Battle of the Plains of Abraham. But the political and financial cost of their participation often seems to be questionable.

Views on the unit known as the Rangers are mixed. They have adopted a more Canadian style of fighting, using cover and crossing country rather than smashing a road through it. From a prototype first set up by John Gorham, Major Robert Rogers is allowed to form a unit of green clad light infantry whose reputation become formidable. Perhaps it becomes dangerously so. Their fortunes are already highly mixed in the field against the French, suffering terrible casualties in one engagement. Their raid on the Abenaki village of St Francis in 1759 combines military futility with an astonishing tale of wilderness survival. Military historians and survivalists amongst our readers might profitably dig further into the background of this astonishing starvation trek through bleak lands.

They might start first with a quick read through of the unit's Standing Orders, 28 rules that simply set out what is required of them. They include - travelling in file, with enough space to avoid two men being killed by the same bullet; crossing soft ground abreast to make tracking harder; rules on sentries at night, and standing to before dawn; using scouts; questioning prisoners separately; when retreating, falling back through the next line that gives covering fire; rallying on high ground; firing from ambush at close distance then charging with hatchets; avoiding using fords or being hemmed in against lakes; ambushing a pursuing enemy by circling back on the path; rules on travelling by boat; and faking a rout in order to turn on the attacker on better ground. The rangers fail militarily when they forget to follow their own rules.

Views of how the locals handle their arms will be dispelled by the 1770s.

Thousands of Loyalists will serve under the King's banners. Butler's Rangers, the British Legion and the Queen's Rangers are just three of the 38 units formed to provide local support. The example and existence of the Boston Association shows how politics is complicated. Perhaps around 19,000 serve in arms, and even that number excludes units such as the non-combatant Black Pioneers. Most are also officered by Loyalists. A number of the more highly valued are made up from recent Highland emigrants, partly there perhaps because they were raised in Halifax early on. Once it becomes clear there is no prospect of a settled peace, albeit rather late in the day, British generals set aside their qualms of exacerbating the politics and enrol more units of local, often dispossessed, volunteers. By now though the outcome is less certain and the risks greater for volunteers. Even so, there is a strong likelihood that you will be sharing your mess with guests from such units, so apply common courtesies.

Military Punishment

The following are some punishments you may be expected to deal with if you are involved as an officer with the courts martial system in the 1770s in America. The punishment awarded is in brackets.

Desertion (500-1500 lashes, or death) - Desertion to rebels (death) - Disguising to leave camp against orders (100 lashes) - Assaulting an officer (1000 lashes) - Unknowingly assaulting an officer, but followed on with insolence and mutiny (800 lashes) - Robbery (500-1000 lashes) - Assisting a robbery (300 lashes) - Robbing from a deceased officer (death) - Robbery from where you are standing guard over (death) - Theft of and killing a town bull (tie to a cart, 100 lashes across town, 3 months imprisonment) - Accidentally mortally wounding a Hessian while firing your musket as an alarm (nil) - Grievous assault on a woman (1000 lashes) - Rape (death) - Plundering (death) - Getting angry and stabbing a soldier in the back with your bayonet (acquit of homicide)

And for officers;

Perjury, slander, improper behaviour in front of soldiers - as a chaplain! (6 months suspended pay and duties) - Quarrelling and fighting with another officer (Ask pardon in front of the regiment gathered under arms; if the commanding officer, a reprimand and 3 month suspension) - Slander against a fellow officer (cashiered) - Killing a soldier in self defence (nil) - Overstating the level of illness being suffered on account of venereal disease to shirk duties (official reprimand from the Divisional Commander) - Taking your men to a tavern while the enemy are 4 or 5 miles away, marauding, and getting drunk on duty (Dismissed on parade, ban from future military employment) - Minor embezzlement of stores (a fine) - Significant military fraud (death)

Note that civilian inhabitants of the garrison, such as wives and servants, are also subject to military law. Lashes are done on the open back, often specified as being done by drummers using Cat of Nine tails, and in cases of large numbers they may be split up into two or more sessions.

Death sentences are often commutable unless the soldier joins the rebels. A lot of cases end in acquittals, so don't assume the result is foregone. Nor is the court invariably biased. Private William

Brown of the 59th Foot for instance gets charged with "having robbed General Howe's Garden on the night of 15th August" (1775), but he's acquitted as he can produce a clear alibi.

"Mercenaries"

Viewing the conflict as akin to a civil war, or even worse as an unwinnable one, a number of British officers decline to accept postings to combat revolutionaries. In 1774, Robert Clive (Clive of India) turns down military command in America. Amherst, who had conquered Canada from the French, declines the same offer in 1775.

Since the Seven Years War, a number of German princes have been contractually available to allow the hiring out of their soldiers to their fellow German princes, the Prince of Hanover (ie the King of Britain) and his ally the King of Prussia. Since the British army isn't huge at the best of times, this proves a convenient way to fill a shortfall in a hurry and has in various forms been shown to work for the past 100 years. It's also, of course, a massive propaganda coup for the rebels, and a concern for those who may be concerned (unjustly as it turns out) at the standards these soldiers will bring with them.

These units, colloquially styled Hessians, are largely from Hessen-Kassel but also from other smaller German states. By and large that means the rulers are part of the extended Hanoverian royal family.

As you know, only the grenadiers wear the pointy hat. You should also recall with caution when you're looking for battlefield targets their tendency to wear blue, just like the Continentals and our artillerymen. Their light infantry or jaeger units by contrast follow the growing custom of wearing green.

There are no Hanoverian soldiers posted here because that country's Estates have banned sending them out of Europe, in part because some postings have high mortality rates from disease. They do get sent elsewhere in Europe to help free up British regiments elsewhere, though you won't see any of them in your American mess.

The reputation of the Germans can't quite be as bad as the rebels are putting about though. At one point, there's even an outlandish proposal by an American diplomat that one German prince should be offered command of the Continental Army in place of Washington. Moreover, a Prussian adventurer by the name of Friedrich von Steuben is accepted when he turns up in 1778 to help sort out a training plan for the Continental Army.

Canada

The French have their own infantry and artillery regiments sent over from Europe, whose style you will be familiar with. There are also the Canadian militia. By the War of 1812, French Canadians are again authorised to participate in formed units and the Voltigeurs are raised in a hurry - rather peculiarly taking their name from a guards unit formed by Napoleon, still Britain's enemy. The officers are members of Quebec's high society, serving under distinguished veteran Charles-Michel de Salaberry. The unit lasts for only three years; is plagued by discipline problems; never becomes more than a militia unit; and yet as we will see goes down in military history.

The Voltigeurs are the key component of the Volunteer Corps. Excluding the red coats, the rest of the local defence force in Lower Canada is made up of a Sedentary Militia (from 1803, every adult under 50 has to train for one weekend a year); and a Select Embodied Militia (a few units of the above on long term call out). The English-speaking militia in Canada are more familiar to the reader established as the Fencible regiments.

Gentlemen and Cheating

A gentleman does not cheat. He should, though, be aware that others might. After the Battle of Hubbardton, an engagement in 1777 that's part of the Ticonderoga/Saratoga campaign, a party of rebels approach British lines with their arms reversed indicating a intent to surrender. Instead though, they ready them and fire before running off.

This is very bad form, as is breaking parole - giving your word to do or not to do something, like try to escape if allowed to walk around and take tea. Thus one can only hold in contempt the attitudes of the rebel leaders after the Battle of the Cedars during the invasion of Canada in 1776; a prisoner exchange is agreed that is reneged upon by Congress on hearing exaggerated tales of savagery by Indian allies (which the British had stepped in to halt, by buying the prisoners from them).

It can get worse. Spies, as is the custom, are shot or potentially hanged. Meanwhile, after the Battle of King's Mountain, Loyalist soldiers attempting to surrender are shot and another ten hanged afterwards. So do not put all your trust in niceties.

Our Top Five Battles

Fort Necessity 1754

Fort Necessity is a tiny stockade in the middle of a slightly marshy field in the middle of nowhere, which is the centre of a skirmish. But its significance is far greater. It is a humiliating training ground for George Washington, the spark of the Seven Years War, the trigger of the final conquest of Canada, the incidental motor for the British Empire expanding into India, and the vacuum that will drain so much revenue and cause the American tax crisis of the 1770s.

The original cause is a clash between two military expeditions to secure competing French and British claims in the Ohio. Washington ambushes a small French party. A junior French officer, there bearing a letter asking the British to depart, is killed by an Indian. Washington returns to the main British force, which sets up some shanty defences. These prove to be no match for the French when they arrive. The defences are sited downhill close by the treeline. The planks making up the wall even splinter when hit by musket fire to create additional injuries (a lesson for the reader there). The trenches in the soggy ground become mires as it rains. The issue looks desperate.

By sheer good fortune, the French get a false report of advancing reinforcements, and decide to offer terms. Washington admits to being guilty for the French officer's death in the surrender document, written in French and using a term that becomes notorious: assassinat. Abandoning their light artillery they march home, leaving the French to burn the place down. Washington returns in 1771 and buys the site, though understandably does not retire there.

Notes for Later Visitors

Fort Necessity National Battlefield comprises three sites - Fort Necessity, Jumonville Glen and Braddock's Grave. Although they represent three different battles, they are all linked to the history of the region and have George Washington as their common thread.

The main unit of the park is located 11 miles east of Uniontown, Pennsylvania on U.S. Highway 40.

Plan 1 1/2 to 2 hrs to see the historic sites in the main unit of the park. Add an hour to visit Braddock's grave and Jumonville Glen sites. These are open during the summer months. The main site is open 9-5 except for certain federal holidays: check http://www.nps.gov/fone/index.htm for details.

Plains of Abraham 1759

The doom of French North America (if we exclude the lingering swamps of Mississippi) falls in Québec. The French have made the best of a bad job by halting the British advance from the east by the Montmorency Falls. Their fire ships have failed to scatter the supporting fleet. Their surprise counter attack succeeded in surprise but failed to attack. Now it is the British commander's turn.

Masterly mingling an understanding both of the current and of lunar phases to limit the moonlight, he sends forces by boat downriver. The sentries, aided by some paltry cries in French, confuse them for an expected (yet as it happens, cancelled) supply shipment. The assault boats land at the base of the key cliffs and start scaling them. They surprise and beat off the slack guard force. Briefly, doubt grips Wolfe and he orders a halt to the mad scramble; his aide-de-camp grips the moment and takes the order to mean a brief pause to reorganise before everyone drags themselves to the summit. By the time the French in the city grasp what has happened, the redcoats and colonial militia are up the cliff and formed up while sailors are already hauling up artillery.

The stage is set. The French swiftly muster their forces from the east. They start to push a wing back, and begin a general advance. The British hold their fire, then discharge a volley at point blank range with each musket charged with two balls. A further volley settles the matter. Both commanders are dying; the city, now open to siege on its exposed western wall, will shortly fall.

New France's fate is not yet completely settled. Quebec in turn faces a winter siege by the French, endured by soldiers and burned-out civilians with much hardship. In 1760, a foray is bloodily repulsed. But as the St Lawrence River thaws, British reinforcements and provisions arrive while France's have been cut off. The British offensive reopens, and Montreal is doomed.

Notes for Later Visitors

The battlefield today is a park lying just outside the city walls, the only remaining eighteenth century fortifications north of the Rio Grande. It has been a preserved site since 1908. Access is straightforward, but we would advise a spot of research and orientation before you go: you might start at the official website, http://www.ccbn-nbc.gc.ca/en/ Wear stout footwear when exploring in winter (this author's boots chose that moment to fall apart).

Yorktown 1781

History has a sense of irony. A few miles from the first enduring British colony at Jamestown, and a few miles again from the old colonial capital of Williamsburg, the American empire effectively comes to an end.

Cornered by larger forces, the British hanker down. Gun emplacements are dug in as entrenchments are hacked out. Cornwallis's supporting flotilla is exposed and either scuppered, burned or driven off.

Cut off by a French fleet from gaining reinforcements or supplies, the British position in Virginia swiftly becomes hopeless. Outnumbered 2:1, they face professional siege engineers and professional artillerymen. The entrenchments cut closer and threaten the eastern positions. Redoubts 9 and 10 are stormed, allowing Washington's artillery to completely dominate British defences. A British sortie damages a battery, but the devastating cannonade continues. Cornwallis resolves to evacuate his force across the river by boat, but a chance storm intercedes.

The British lines are wracked with malaria. The only option left is to capitulate. Cornwallis sends his deputy, O'Hara; he is invited to surrender to Washington's deputy, Lincoln. The redcoats march out to the field of surrender. The world is turned upside down.

Notes for Later Visitors

Yorktown enjoys the advantage of being a major battlefield park and has an excellent visitor's centre. A number of artillery pieces from the period are on the site, helping to add to the atmosphere.

The York River has significantly eroded the original bank, resulting in the loss of a large part of one of the key redoubts (10). The original earthworks were subsequently reused by the Confederate Army during a later siege, generating some changes as the Union forces entrenched in Washington's lines. So a part of what you see today is reconstruction on the original site. The Moore House where the articles of capitulation were signed has survived, though.

The Visitor Centre is open 9-5 though most of the year, and the park closes at sunset. Check for details on http://www.nps.gov/york/index.htm

The Capture of USS Chesapeake 1813

A frigate of the era.

Some of the greatest excitement to be found takes place not on land but at sea, as the fledgling United States navy engages in a series of encounters with the mighty Royal Navy.

Well, not quite. Vast amounts of naval warfare involves small privateers from Bermuda or Halifax or Boston, putting out to sea and having a go at weak trading vessels flying the other's flag to capture them as prizes; or small ships of either side running into big ships and being taken apart by them. The US may not have any ships of the line, but its design of frigates makes them a match of counterparts supposedly of the same calibre.

This is why the fight between the Chesapeake and the Shannon, Captains Lawrence versus Broke, is particularly - excuse the pun - engaging, since for once the two combatants are of relatively equal strength. Even better, if you get on one of the spectating small boats that bob dangerously close to the action or clamber onto a harbourside rooftop, you might be able to wrangle a view.

The Chesapeake has been in the news before. In 1807, it received several broadsides from HMS Leopard after declining to allow the Royal Navy to come aboard to remove some deserters. That triggered an apology and compensation payment. This might be considered a grudge match. Chesapeake has more guns than the Shannon, but the latter's crew has had more time at sea and in gun training.

Chesapeake flies the banner that reflects the key grievances of the War of 1812: Free Trade and Sailors (the catchiness and meaning loses a lot with the passage of time). The vessels go alongside one another, firing broadsides. The two ships collide, and both sides set to a hand-to-hand struggle. The mortal wound of the American captain proves critical. All American officers still on deck are hors de combat. Broke meanwhile is badly wounded but survives. The Chesapeake strikes its flag. It's taken back as prize to Halifax, to serve its final years as HMS Chesapeake.

Lawrence's final words, "Don't give up the ship", thus prove to be unfulfilled, but do enter American naval legend. Controversy remains though whether he should have taken his raw crew out to sea after barely arriving in post himself, with morale reportedly low (owing to lack of pay), orders to avoid combat, and throwing away the advantage of being upwind. But you can judge the reality behind those claims by watching events for yourself.

Notes for Later Visitors

Captain Lawrence and his First Lieutenant were originally originally interred at the Old Saint Paul Burying Ground in Halifax, but were removed under a flag of truce in 1813 – after a spell in Salem, Lawrence now lies at Trinity Church in New York. Other British officers remain though at that location. Halifax's Naval Museum holds the Shannon's bell, which was cracked during the engagement. See http://psphalifax.ca/marcommuseum/index.html for directions.

Those interested in learning more about life at sea will enjoy a trip to the historic dockyard at Portsmouth. There is enough here to easily fill an entire day, extending well beyond the period covered in this book (it famously hosts the Mary Rose). Once the main museum complex is fully reopened it will complement what is already on offer from a tour of HMS Victory. For more details, see http://www.historicdockyard.co.uk/

Victory of course is not a frigate. To better appreciate how the engagement may have felt, we suggest a visit to USS Constitution in Boston. Chesapeake's sister ship had better fortune, though easier battles: find out more on http://www.history.navy.mil/ussconstitution/ Two slightly later RN frigates from the 1820s also survive in Hartlepool and Dundee: see http://www.hms-trincomalee.co.uk/ and http://www.frigateunicorn.org/

Or you can go and see the original Chesapeake. Just like the mediaeval cogs that were turned into supporting pillars in the Tower of London, the original beams were salvaged when the vessel was taken apart. They were used to build a flour mill in the Hampshire village of Wickham. Today it's a Grade II listed building, a shop and a cafe: to plan a stop off, see http://www.chesapeakemill.co.uk/ The decking is largely as lifted from the original vessel. See if you can spot the blood stains.*

Chateauguay 1813

In autumn 1813, a major American push on Canada looks set to overwhelm Montreal and seize the economic heartland of Canada. Taking the city would also isolate all British units in Upper Canada, already hard pressed after the loss of much of the Great Lakes. A column of 3,000 Americans is advancing over a barrage of hastily laid obstacles. As it comes to the Chateauguay River, it hits the resistance.

Lt Col de Salaberry has placed his far smaller force in the best defensive positions possible. Making use of woods, undulating terrain and swampy land, his forces block the enemy's advance. An American flanking force pushes forward on the south side of the river, only to run into a reinforced detachment which routs them and pushes them back level with the main body. Meanwhile, the main American advance begins. A militia unit gives ground, but as the Americans think the battle is theirs, Salaberry orders a cacophony of noise and bugles across the front. With the limited visibility, the Americans are confused and their assault weakens. Meanwhile, the Canadian attack south of the river hits stronger American resistance and they are forced back again. The pursuing Americans in turn emerge from the treeline and find that some Canadian forces north of the river have been sited to overlook them, and they take damaging flanking fire driving them back. The southern force retreats in disorder; the northern force withdraws after them. The Canadians – no British are involved - have won.

Notes for Later Visitors

This battle ranks, perhaps with Vimy, as one of the key formative events in Canadian military and even national history and identity. The area today is a national historic site, and run by Parks Canada. It's best visited when most open, June to September, or weekends into October. Details are on

http://www.pc.gc.ca/lhn-nhs/qc/chateauguay/index.aspx There's an interpretive centre and a trail: you may wish to bring a bike!

The other key battle that occurred in conjunction with this invasion, and equally celebrated, is that of Crysler's Farm. The Anglo-Canadian force is outnumbered over 3:1, but beats off the attackers. The site today lies between Brockville and Montreal on the 401 (Macdonald-Cartier Freeway), seven miles east of Morrisburg. A lot of the land was lost to the St Lawrence Seaway – the memorial itself was moved to its present site. There is a visitor's centre, open for much of May to the end of August: details here - http://www.uppercanadavillage.com/index.cfm/en/activities/daily-programs/battle-of-cryslers-farm-visitor-centre/

Chapter 6
Meet and Greet

High Season 1700-1763

Let's start our tour of people you may drop in on with the French colonies, since these are at their apogée at this time. Antoine Laumet de la Mothe Cadillac (1658-1730), is an early settler of the hinterland of the north. He was born in Gascony, and despite his pretended title is not actually of the nobility so don't quiz him too closely on that. Don't ask him too much about his military experience either as this is also a bit ropey. By 1700, he has already been in New France for a couple of decades, so is an old hand. He has a bad reputation in his home area of Acadie, but after his home is wrecked by the English colonists he gets taken under the wing of Québec's governor - the charming, unscrupulous and now late Louis de Buade de Frontenac (1622-1698) - and has found himself posted out west near the hub of the three western Great Lakes. This proves an ideal opportunity to make money, not all perhaps appropriately. Cadillac spots the potential for further development, and right now has just got the agreement of the King of France to form part of a team that sets up what will become Detroit, whose management he subsequently takes over. Accept his bribes if you will, but don't get too attached to him; in 1710 he is appointed to the exile post of governorship of empty Louisiana, which he only bothers to go to in 1713. After a mixed term there, he's recalled to France and spends a stint in the Bastille, though emerges back in favour and ends up in small town French administration.

Compare Cadillac with a native-born explorer, Pierre Gaultier de Varennes et de la Vérendrye. He's from Trois-Rivières, the son of an officer who came over with the celebrated Carignan Regiment. After schooling with the Jesuits, de la Vérendrye serves for a while in the army in France. Following a spell in farming, he joins his siblings in the fur trade. From 1731, he's given a charter to explore north west of the Great Lakes, setting up several important outposts but not reaching the sea. After this period, don't discuss how his family is faring on these trips, as several, including his son, are murdered or die of illness. By 1742, he has discovered the Rockies, but can go no further. He never gets to reach the further oceans, and while he is honoured locally by some, his discoveries are barely credited at Versailles.

Or there's Pierre-Esprit Radisson. By 1700 he's been exploring Canada for a half century. Usefully for us, he failed to get the proper licence and had his furs confiscated by his government back in the 1660s. Since then he's been working with English traders instead; indeed, his discovery of copper ore led to the establishment of the Hudson Bay Company. After a stint back on the French books, followed by coming back again to English employment, we think he's now retired on a HBC pension. You might be able to track him down in London before you go.

Pierre le Moyne d'Iberville (1661-1706) is an example of French Canada's lost potential. Catch him at the outset of your visit as he is not around for long. He's from a wealthy family, originally from Dieppe but made (very) good by outstanding contacts with the Indians. His small naval expeditions against English outposts during the wars demonstrated an astonishing ability, applying Canadien tactics long used on land to the sea. His finest moments are at the helm of his famous ship the Pélican with which he became the terror of the Hudson Bay. Now with peace come, he follows up the work done by explorer René-Robert Cavelier (de La Salle - d.1687) to secure France's claims on Louisiana by establishing key forts. His footprint on the New World further spreads with the outbreak of further fighting, as he ravages the West Indies. His demise at Havana due to illness removes a resourceful enemy. Be cautious when discussing his children, as an illegitimate daughter triggered a maintenance case in his youth. Also be prudent when discussing his brothers, who are as talented as he is (one is off-and-on governor of Louisiana and founds New Orleans and Mobile), but have a high mortality rate in fighting. Don't trust him in war, as in a conflict in the frozen north he refused a gentlemen's agreement to allow hunting to avoid scurvy, and took a surgeon prisoner on a false parole. Don't introduce him to any Newfoundlanders, since he has cruelly ravaged that island's communities. Note also that by now he has severe malaria, so he may not turn up as invited if stricken by a bout. After his death, some irregularities on his last campaign badly dent the reputation of his surviving family, which may affect the seating arrangements at any dinner party you may be planning to throw.

Marie-Marguerite d' Youville (1701-1771) reminds us that there is more to New France than explorers, fur traders and soldiers. Widowed aged 30, with only two out of six children surviving (they would become priests), this saintly lady devoted herself to charity and to looking after the destitute. In 1737, she and some associates organised themselves into the Sisters of Charity of Montreal, the "Grey Nuns". She has dedicated herself to the cause ever since.

Then there are the Acadiens. A key figure here is Joseph Broussard. He is a key figure of the Acadian resistance. For several years he fights on, until the end of New France. It's hard to see how he can keep his smile, and the upbeat temperament that gains him the nickname of 'Beausoleil'. That's a side of him the victims of his Indian allies can hardly suspect. He ends his days choosing exile in Louisiana with his family. Perhaps one day one of his descendents may become even more globally famous than he, reflecting as Destiny's Child on the Best Thing I Never Had.

New France's sunset personalities scrap over control. The Marquis de Vaudreuil is the governor, indeed the son of a former governor making it a family affair. However, he is closely associated with his superintendant of finances, François Bigot, whose years (in a post he seems not to want to stay in) become indelibly marked with every form of imaginable embezzlement, depriving the weak colony of key resources needed to develop and protect it. Perhaps he might have emerged with some credit if he hadn't been part of the team that lost Canada. Vaudreuil himself sees the military appointment of the Marquis de Montcalm as a subsidiary position. The orders that come with the general and his scanty reinforcements do not help matters, and Montcalm himself seeks greater control. The tension between the two over strategy, and the split command between colonial and French forces, exacerbate the difficulties of defence and it

is a wonder Montcalm is able to deliver any victories at all. Perhaps the general is his own worst enemy and indisposed by character to understand the conditions of the settlers rather than the strategic role the Canadian diversion might play. His death at Québec simplifies the command structure, and creates a punch line for the jokes of the Paris set: "J'ai perdu mon calme." As for the survivors, Vaudreuil's son goes on to conquer Senegal, takes part in the naval campaign off the Chesapeake, and tries to defend Louis XVI at the Tuileries in 1792 (faring better than the massacred Swiss Guard). Montcalm's subordinate, the young Louis-Antoine de Bougainville, has astonishingly just been elected a Fellow of the Royal Society in London, and later he too shifts to the French navy. He is thwarted in an attempt to settle the Falklands with Acadien exiles, is seemingly the first Frenchman to circumnavigate the globe, and is another New France connection found at the Chesapeake.

This era is famous for the redcoat commanders these men will face. There are a number of obvious candidates you might veer towards. Less well known than his junior Wolfe (whose uncertain track record is salvaged by his victory and death), we would recommend dropping by to see General Jeffery Amherst (1717-1797). Amherst's seen action in the thick of the War of the Austrian Succession, and served alongside the Hessians. Although quite junior, he gets a surprise acting promotion and is sent over to sort out the capture of Louisbourg. A few months later, he is promoted to land commander of the whole theatre, which ends in success. You might question his ethics if you believe the reports as true about him agreeing to blankets infected with smallpox being passed on to hostile Indians. The tactic is not new: there are suggestions of it being used against the Cherokee 25 years earlier, and the French had a notion there was a plot to wipe out the Micmacs too - but it's not clear if the suggestion reportedly put to him was carried out and in any event, the outbreak was already in the area. Amherst returns to Europe and to other postings, though turns down two offers to take command of British forces during the American rebellion. Why not drop by at his home at Sevenoaks, called Montreal House?

A rather different cut is made by Sir William Johnson, the so-called "Mohawk baronet". This astonishing Anglo-Irishman sets out running a family estate, then resolves to understand the language, ways and customs of the neighbouring Iroquois. Innovative, he seizes the opportunity to become a key figure in the local fur trade. His skills are officially recognised as he becomes the colonial intermediary, gaining local neutrality and then mobilising support during the Seven Years War. He is the constant link securing the Mohawk alliance, which he also makes use of to become a land baron. In discussions, don't bring up his family first, as he has rather unorthodox relations. Do ask him some tips on how to deal with the Indians.

His advice is useful for example in ending the stalemated war with the old French ally, the Ottawa chief Pontiac (d. 1767). An eminent strategist capable of bridging tribal divides, Pontiac is able to organise a concurrent mass attack on scattered outposts. He rejects colonial expansion, and even regrets it seems the loss of traditional bows and arrows. Treat him with respect, since that is what he seeks the most. Another fascinating native is the Iroquois chief Canassatego. This Onondonga leader in 1744 contributes to the Lancaster deliberations some ideas that surprise the colonial delegates on how his people manage political confederation. He holds little truck for the colonial education of his fellows, who thus forget how to hunt, build cabins, and turn out to be rubbish counsellors: instead, he offers to train

A spirited painting of the last fight of Blackbeard the Pirate, who was a curse along the Atlantic coast of America.

and educate a dozen of the colonists' sons in his people's ways! Despite expressing concerns about his people's reliance on outside trade, he has some rather fine European clothing. He is such a hit, Franklin even publishes a compilation of his speeches. He is tall, well-built, engaging, with a commanding presence, though when you're most likely to meet him he'll be in old age.

Someone you should avoid, however, is Edward Teach, better known as Blackbeard. He has a penchant for drama, with pistols stuck into his belt and gunpowder sizzling from the braids of his beard as his gives you a broadside from the deck of the Queen Anne's Revenge. He profits from a royal pardon to settle in the Carolinas, but such a quiet life is not for him and with the collusion of thc local governor, he is back to his old habits. Not for long. It's hard to distinguish myth from reality; in this case, we suggest you don't chance it and keep clear of his infamous flag (but if he's hoisted it, it's already too late). Still, if you've got ransom money, you'll probably make it out alive.

> And whereas several Pyrates roving up and down the American seas, as well Northern as Southern, do much damnifie trade and molest the subjects of both crowns in their navigation and commerce in those parts, it is agreed that strict orders should be given to the Governors and officers of both kings, that they give no assistance or protection to any Pyrates of what nation soever, nor suffer them to have any retreat in the ports or roads of their respective Government.
>
> Text of the 1686 Treaty of Whitehall (from an official translation from the Latin copied in the 1720s)

Mid Season 1763-1783

The opportunities for meeting astonishing characters does not diminish with the removal of the French dimension. Indeed, there's a positive flowering of political genius - some planted from abroad.

We begin with Thomas Paine (1737-1809). After unsatisfactory service in Customs and Excise, he emigrates to America. In early

1776 he publishes the critically important pamphlet Common Sense, arguing for independence and a republic. This is remarkably widely read: it even gets an audience in England, and a censored version is circulated in France. Paine follows this with The American Crisis, a series of short essays produced during the conflict. The first one is perhaps the most influential, and its opening line amongst the most famous;

THESE are the times that try men's souls. The summer soldier and the sunshine patriot will, in this crisis, shrink from the service of their country; but he that stands by it now, deserves the love and thanks of man and woman. Tyranny, like hell, is not easily conquered; yet we have this consolation with us, that the harder the conflict, the more glorious the triumph. What we obtain too cheap, we esteem too lightly: it is dearness only that gives everything its value.

Avoid discussing his schooling and early life (a series of failures) or jokes about clothing (his father made corsets). Steer clear of politics – he gets fired during the revolution for leaking word on a political scandal. Do ask him about his future plans for inventions such as a new design of crane, and a huge iron bridge (one gets built in Sunderland). Having returned to the very England he had urged sedition against, Paine and Edmund Burke will famously later cross swords over the French Revolution, with Paine penning The Rights of Man in 1791. This, while popular, upsets the censors and Paine sensibly flees the country. He is, ironically, then arrested by the Jacobins after defending the moderate Girondins, and writes The Age of Reason attacking organised religion while stuck in a French jail. He returns to the United States to find himself considered too radical for the political elite, and dies shortly afterwards.

You might find such freedom to travel unusual given the Revolution. But consider the case of John Barker Church. During the Revolution he actually supplies the Revolutionary army and the French one. After the war he returns to his native England where he becomes a Member of Parliament for a while!

A fellow inventor of course is Benjamin Franklin (1706-1790), who invents the lightning rod after experimenting with becoming one while flying a kite during a storm (and is rather fortunate to survive), as well as creating bifocals. He's from a printing family which has a tradition of taking on authority. He makes his name by turning the Pennsylvania Gazette into an important paper. Even more remarkable is the vast array of public works he pushes or supports, such as subscription libraries, fire brigades, fire insurance, and a hospital. He waives a patent on his design of stove, considering it a common good.

Over the better part of two decades, you can visit Franklin in London, which he loves. He's appointed the Colonial Representative by no fewer than four colonies by the end of his time there: he'll leave in 1774. If visiting Paris before you go to America, you might bump into him there during the revolution. Do make the effort; he has a good sense of humour and is excellent company.

Franklin's an early advocate of colonial union in some form, though it's hard to say at what point he becomes a full supporter of independence so that might make an interesting discovery. Be cautious in discussing his private life, as he has a child before he marries (who becomes a Loyalist governor, and the two fall out). Do ask about some of the turns of phrase he is said to have invented in one of his almanacks, such as 'a penny saved is a penny earned'.

The viewpoint of John Adams (1735-1826) is rather plainer. An outspoken advocate of a total rupture with Britain, he is one of only a handful for whom no potential pardon is authorised as part of any deal. Energetic, self-assured, you might find him a little puffed up perhaps at times. He'll advance to be the minister to France and then to Britain, Vice President, and then succeed Washington to become the second President. If visiting, make a point of chatting to his son, John Quincy Adams (b. 1767) who has an interest in politics too. As a child he was a spectator of Bunker Hill. He may test his languages out on you.

Adams Senior is succeeded in turn by a political rival but old associate, the defender of states' rights Thomas Jefferson (1743-1836). Jefferson is a must-visit during your stay, whether on holiday or leading a troop of cavalry. The Virginian is lanky, an eloquent writer but an indifferent public speaker. He adds fire and gold to the scripts of independence, and measure to its design. He is later very sympathetic to the French revolutionaries, another factor that generates rifts with the opposing Federalist camp seeking a stronger central government. The original peculiar electoral system means that he becomes Adams's Vice President while having stood against him; and then four years later is at the centre of a bigger political crisis following a tied election, which Jefferson wins to become President. If you visit him in retirement, raise a discussion on his plans to found a university in his state. As a singular quirk of fate, both Jefferson and Adams will die on the 50th anniversary to the day of the signing of the Declaration of Independence.

Amongst all these political titans we must not forget our Zeuses. There are numerous Loyalists whose memory will be eclipsed by events, but who are contributing importantly to the current political debate. Thomas Paine's work for instance is countered by James Chalmers (1727-1806), a Maryland resident. His essay, Plain Truth, written under the pseudonym of 'Candidus', sets out to defend the British constitution "which with all its imperfections, is, and ever will be the pride and envy of mankind." He concludes that "independence and slavery are synonymous terms". The problem is though that he is not as eloquent as Paine. Chalmers subsequently joins a Loyalist regiment, and is forced at the close to leave his country.

Joseph Galloway (1731-1803) is a statesman who almost changes the entire course of world history. A Pennsylvania delegate to the First Continental Congress, his proposed compromise misses being adopted by a single vote. Tellingly, it is later erased from the records. He joins the Loyalist camp and runs Philadelphia while it is secured, then is forced to withdraw to England. Galloway sees the push for American taxation as perfectly reasonable given the millions that Britain has spent in the American interest. He underlines that the very existence of the colonies in the first place was established by the British Crown. He is also horrified by the prospect of a terrible civil war.

Galloway has married extremely well, and has strong support from the Quaker community from which he originates. In his local assembly, he gets on well with Franklin, and ends up as Speaker. He supports the embargo on British imports, so don't expect him to be blindly sympathetic. Don't discuss his house, which gets confiscated and auctioned off after the rebels declare him a traitor, while his wife's own estate is being legally fought over: as he's forced into exile and she is ailing, he'll never see her again.

Galloway is not the only delegate who refuses to sign the Declaration of Independence. Other Loyalists you may be interested in hearing their side of the story from include John Dickinson of Pennsylvania and James Duane, Robert Livingston and John Jay of New York. Four delegates - Carter Braxton of Virginia, Robert Morris of Pennsylvania, George Reed of Delaware, and Edward

Rutledge of South Carolina - are opposed, but sign in order not to show disunity. Many will end up as leading Federalists after the Revolution, supporting a unified central government to replace the Crown and to maintain order.

Dickinson's case is particularly notable as he had been key in opposing the Stamp Act ten years before. He is not an optimist on what an independent America might bring, and considers from personal experience that London still has much to offer. He looks a little thin and flaky, and be understanding as he has gout. A reserved individual, he is horrified by the aggressive and belligerent mood in New England and surprises the more extreme of his colleagues by not sharing in it. In a debate pushing for a second Olive Branch petition, tempers get so heated half of Congress walks out. He is no friend of Adams, thanks to an intemperate letter of the latter that gets captured by the British and published. The exasperation is extended as Dickinson holds out the longest against complete rupture, and the new revolutionary government in his own colony sacks him as their delegate. He is later reinstated, and continues to contribute significantly to constitutional development, but his star is not as high.

But let's turn now to some key characters on the military side. Pre-eminent naturally is the man who will become the head of the Continental forces, George Washington (1732-1799). Much has been written of him already, so suffice it to point to a few snares. Washington is very much a gentleman of the old school, so do stick to form. From what we have seen he is a customarily brave officer, coming close to injury or death during the French war, but not a particularly inspired one tactically. His importance comes in two aspects. Firstly, he has a good strategic appreciation of needs and opportunities, especially in keeping his army in one piece and maintaining just enough morale through the tricky periods. His masterly use of deception keeps British reinforcements from relieving the embattled forces at Yorktown. He is also inspiring through example, and this is especially important after the war. He is able to quash a mutiny by personal appeal to his officers and seemingly through a display of his own frailty (simply by pulling out a pair of spectacles). Washington's character, it might be said, preserves the rebellion by failing to have his army destroyed, and preserves the United States from becoming an autocracy in place of a monarchy. An easy slur to avoid is to refuse to recognise his Continental rank and call him "Mr".

Contrast with Henry "Light Horse Harry" Lee (1756-1818). He rises through the ranks to command a cavalry unit that plays a significant part of the war of manoeuvre. Washington admires his dash. We think some of it may have rubbed off on his son, young Robert E. Lee (b. 1807). Sadly, his later life is marred by the untimely death of his wife, and financial difficulties that lead to a spell in prison. He dies perhaps through the enduring injuries from being beaten up by an angry Baltimore mob that was out to lynch a friend. Naval types might be more interested to speak to John Paul Jones (1747-1792). An absconding merchant sailor, you will view him as a pirate. That said, he is a brave one. The report of his brutality towards a member of his crew did not stand up in court, so give him the benefit of the doubt on that score. Don't expect him to honour any invitation to visit you in England, where his name is mud; and don't ask him how his future prospects are turning out with the post-war navy, as his expected command of a major warship never happens. On the other hand, his experiences fighting for the Russians provide a few arresting tales.

Two foreign gentlemen may also be worthy of your attention. The first is the ridiculously young Lafayette (1757-1834) on whom equally we need add little. Ironically, his interest in America is piqued by a conversation with George III's brother. He invests in his own private warship, accepts a foreign commission in the Continental Army, and goes off to war. His persistence leads to massive acclaim in Europe, which might be irksome to his American colleagues so be wary of ascribing victory just to him as the 'guiding European' who is involved. His later pursuit of revolutionary ideas back home is even more interesting; as the French Revolution unfurls, he pushes for defined human rights, and perhaps plays a hand in establishing the new national colours and flag (the monarchy's white added to Paris's blue and red). It's Lafayette who sends Washington the key to the Bastille after it's been stormed, transported on part of its journey by Paine. As commander of the National Guard, he for a while is able to save the Royal Family, but has to flee to the Austrian Netherlands where he spends some years in prison. American diplomatic intervention years later gets him released. He re-enters politics after Napoleon's abdication, and will participate in yet another

revolution in 1830 to overthrow Charles X.

The Prussian adventurer Baron von Steuben (1730-1794) profits considerably from a misunderstanding about his service and rank. Even his social background was invented by a relative. As a result, he ends up as the drill master for the Continentals at Valley Forge, a role it turns out he is able to achieve highly effectively despite his weak mastery of English and his group arriving in the country in misjudged red uniforms! You can tell he's near by the arrival of his pet greyhound, and by the swearing. He is subsequently given a field command, and plays a key role in demobilisation after the war. If meeting him then, be forewarned that he is heavily in debt so do not expect grandiose treatment. He is also under attack thanks to the new Society of the Cincinnati. Von Steuben becomes a prominent member of its Order, and a visible head of its New York Chapter. This is an organisation open to officers who have served in the war; but crucially, membership is also meant to be passed onto their descendants. This makes it an hereditary honour, something some Americans having abolished the nobility are nervous about. It's also quite obviously a lobby group campaigning about overdue back pay, which makes it a dangerous political force. In its defence, a French Society for allied senior ranks and Continental officers is also set up, and it also acts as a fund to help orphans and war widows. We suspect the long term threat is overplayed. But given the tenor of this tome, leave this volume behind if you go to his office. Also, don't ask why only officers are allowed into the club.

Ethan Allen (1738-1789) heads up a more rag tag force, Vermont's Green Mountain Boys. He plays an important part at the very outset, though you'll be able to chat to him in captivity when he's taken prisoner at Montreal. On release, he becomes a central figure in the political shenanigans over the future of the Vermont Republic, whose residents are in a longstanding turf war with the government of New York. It even transpires there are negotiations as to whether they might get a better deal rejoining the British Empire, though judging by the treatment of Loyalists in the region this seems to be high stakes brinksmanship. It appears to work, since Vermont ends up as the 14th state. Allen also has the good sense to steer clear of Daniel Shays' tax rebellion, which threatens to expand and ignite the controversy.

Benedict Arnold's Loyalties

Benedict Arnold (1741-1801) is one of the heroes of the early Revolution. He plays a role in the capture of Fort Ticonderoga, though the Green Mountain Boys get drunk on the stockpiled rum and abuse him. His expenses don't get fully paid. His expedition to Quebec ends in defeat and military disputes over lost stores. His promotion is limited. He plays a key part in saving the First Battle of Saratoga, but doesn't get the credit. He gets court martialed for improper use of transport. His new wife is friends with British spy master Major John André. The dynamics create themselves: he switches sides.

In 1780, he writes a letter to a colonial newspaper explaining his defection to the Loyalist cause. Some accuse him of venality, others of succumbing to his Loyalist wife, others of simply being subject to powerful enemies in rebel circles. Yet whatever the reality, this letter usefully explores the complexities of the tugging loyalties and interests in play across a broader part of the population. A short extract suffices;

"I lamented, therefore, the impolicy, tyranny, and injustice, which, with a sovereign contempt of the people of America, studiously neglected to take their collective sentiments of the British proposals of peace, and to negociate, under a suspension of arms, for an adjustment of differences; I lamented it as a dangerous sacrifice of the great interests of this country to the partial views of a proud, ancient, and crafty foe. I had my suspicions of some imperfections in our councils, on proposals prior to the Parliamentary Commission of 1778; but having then less to do in the Cabinet than the field (I will not pronounce peremptorily, as some may, and perhaps justly, that Congress have veiled them from the public eye), I continued to be guided in the negligent confidence of a Soldier. But the whole world saw, and all America confessed, that the overtures of the second Commission exceeded our wishes and expectations; and if there was any suspicion of the national liberality, it arose from its excess."

[Some words on the French we here pass by]

With the highest satisfaction I bear testimony to my old fellow soldiers and citizens, that I find solid ground to rely upon the clemency of our Sovereign, and abundant conviction that it is the generous intention of Great Britain not only to leave the rights and privileges of the colonies unimpaired, together with their perpetual exemption from taxation, but to superadd such further benefits as may consist with the common prosperity of the empire. In short, I fought for much less than the parent country is as willing to grant to her colonies as they can be to receive or enjoy.

Some may think I continued in the struggle of these unhappy days too long, and others that I quitted it too soon.-- To the first I reply, that I did not see with their eyes, nor perhaps had so favourable a situation to look from, and that to our common master I am willing to stand or fall. In behalf of the candid among the latter, some of whom I believe serve blindly but honestly--in the bands I have left, I pray God to give them all the lights requisite to their own safety before it is too late; and with respect to that herd of censurers, whose enmity to me originates in their hatred to the principles by which I am now led to devote my life to the re-union of the British empire, as the best and only means to dry up the streams of misery that have deluged this country, they may be assured, that, conscious of the rectitude of my intentions, I shall treat their malice and calumnies with contempt and neglect.

New York, October 7, 1780. B. Arnold

What of the British officers, with whom you are more likely to socialise at this time? General John Burgoyne (1722-1792) went to school with General Gage. His nickname is "Gentleman Johnny" because of his interest in high fashion. He's a gambler, and indeed eloped with his wife after her father refused permission to marry. It's risk taking that fails to pay off in the Saratoga campaign, where he decides to push on rather than withdraw back along his supply line. After the war, he'll become a leading society figure, and continue to write plays good enough to be performed.

There are two surviving Howes in this campaign (George Howe dying at Ticonderoga in 1758). General William Howe (1729-1814) is a veteran of the French war. Sympathetic to colonial arguments, he advocates the reversal of the tax policy. In the end, he accepts a senior posting during the revolution. The casualties at Bunker Hill push him into a caution that hampers the direction of the war, for instance by failing to push on Washington when he's cornered outside of New York. He allows himself to be distracted by the prize of Philadelphia rather than supporting the increasingly outnumbered Burgoyne. On the positive side, he throws a fine party. His brother is Admiral Richard Howe (1728-1799), who shares his views on the merits of the colonial case on taxes, and knows Franklin. As commander of the naval forces, he joins his brother in peace feelers at Staten Island. He cuts short his posting owing to political disagreements. He suffered a head injury from the French some years back so perhaps you might avoid discussing wigs; or, given the Tory Government, Whigs. Also, don't question him about his part in Anson's 1740 raid on South America - as Howe's ship fails to get past the Cape so he neither gets a share of the immense booty nor manages to circumnavigate the world.

Then there is General Charles Cornwallis (1738-1805). Cornwallis is rather more professional than some of his colleagues, taking the art of war seriously. Like the Howes, he too is sympathetic to the colonials, and as a member of the House of Lords opposed the tax legislation. He is a very competent commander, but plagued by a shortage of troops and, while operating in the south, malaria. He is also confronted with unconventional warfare, or as we gentlemen know it, cheating. His march on Virginia results in Pyrrhic victories, some narrow failures to seize major strategic successes, and being bottled up by a combination of bad luck, atrocious weather, and clever rebel manoeuvring. By a twist of fate, he negotiates surrender to the son of the man who - as Constable of the Tower of London - he is holding prisoner in London. He later has better luck putting down an Irish rebellion and defeating the celebrated Tipu Sultan in India.

Cornwallis does not get on at all with his immediate superior who takes over from Howe, General William Clinton (1730-1795), especially as the two clash over overall strategy and Clinton sees resources being dragged away from the north. Clinton's associated with the continent through his father, a past royal governor, and he himself grew up in New York and started his military service in the militia. We're not quite sure what useful techniques he picked up from his study tour of the Russian army before coming here, but he's

It is best not to talk to James Madison about religion, you will never get away once he starts on the subject.

promoted to become the third overall commander after Gage and Howe, the latter of whom he blames for failing to capture the Continentals at New York. Clinton's preference for a war of manoeuvre, backed by the fleet, fares better than head on assaults but by now is undermined by the French threat to the Caribbean and the presence of their forces in the theatre. Clinton in turn is replaced by Guy Carleton (1724-1808, later Lord Dorchester). Now he really is a man you should meet.

A friend of Wolfe, Carleton serves with him during the Quebec campaign. This is the start of a very long association with Canada. Carleton will be subsequently appointed the conquered colony's Lieutenant Governor, holds onto a newly-won territory with a small garrison, and is key to securing favourable status for the colony on the eve of the revolution. By opening up to local notables and winning the consent if not the support of the Catholic Church, encouraging local manufactures, restoring many aspects of the French legal code, and backing Indian hunting rights, he stabilises the local political scene. Come the Revolution, he holds onto the province and repels the rebel attack. After Clinton's fall from favour, he is sent out again as Commander in Chief of what's left in 1782, which to his displeasure means managing the extrication of redcoats, Loyalists and escaped slaves before New York is handed over. He does this with considerable skill and considerable honour, expanding further his existing reputation as a humane administrator. Later, he returns to Quebec as governor of what's left of British North America. If he is rather proconsular in his approach, that is exactly his job, and he gets things on a firm setting under a new constitutional arrangement in 1791. Perhaps we might say that he is the founding father of Canada. Don't be put off if he comes across as stand-offish, even in a social setting. He's certainly extremely guarded, but he has cause to be: all the more so in later life after a leaked letter causes a diplomatic incident.

If Carleton embodies Canadian continuity, Sir Robert Eden (1741-1784) perhaps represents a political form of apostolic succession. A soldier, he marries the sister of Lord Baltimore, who owns Maryland. This catapults him into the post of governor. His amiability and social outgoingness wins him many friends. He is a leading light in the local scene (find him at the Homony Club, founded in 1770 and named after a dish of mushy corn). It is not enough to keep him in post come the Revolution, and in June 1776 after a period in office but not in power he is formally encouraged to leave, notably in this instance with his possessions. On arriving in England he is made a baronet of Maryland while the Baltimore inheritance is fought over in the courts. In 1783, he returns to Annapolis to assist a relative in some legal claims. By fortuitous timing, the last Royal Governor of Maryland is thus present in the capital building (of which he had laid the cornerstone) to witness George Washington resign command of the army before the Continental Congress. He dies a few months later, but we expect the Eden family will produce more members who will have interesting American political connections.

A different kind of noble is Joseph Brant (1742-1807), known to his people as Thayendanegea. A Mohawk chief, he is also an aide to an Anglican missionary, and a commander of his people during the war. Not many war leaders can claim to have translated a gospel into Iroquois. His community work leads to him travelling to England, and he meets the King, cementing his loyalist tendencies. But his allies are defeated and he leads his people to exile in Canada. A measure of his success in further lobbying is North America's only chapel royal, St Paul's or the "Chapel of the Mohawks" to replace the one they had lost. If you encounter him there, you may find him poring over one of his further translations of key Christian texts.

Low Season 1783-1815

The Low Season sees opportunities to visit the new republic in a period of political effervescence (approaching occasionally on disorder) and – mostly – peace. It also sees the establishment of a group of colonies to the north set in a political mirror, since they provide continuity with the old order and maintain their links with the mother land. So who might you decide to track down at this time?

While Joseph Brant is engaged in re-establishing his kindred, a famous counterpart of his is engaged in defending his people's rights by war. Tecumseh (1768-1813) is a Shawnee chief who leads the fight against encroachments on his people's land in Ohio. Son of a chief killed in battle on the eve of the Revolutionary War, he spends the following years engaged in frontier fighting and refuses to accept peace when it finally comes. One of his brothers emerges as a prophet figure, his reputation sealed when he predicts an eclipse. This gives him star attraction and leads to the establishment of a proto-capital, Prophetstown. It's Tecumseh who becomes the key political figure though. The United States views the emerging grand confederacy as a threat, especially if war with Britain breaks out, and marches against it in 1811. His dream is broken, and he dies as conflict expands into the War of 1812. Tecumseh is a fascinating individual, brave, generous, widely admired, and a good public speaker. His idealism points to an alternative nation in North America that falls short of coming to pass. He is definitely on your must-visit list.

Tecumseh's key ally is Sir Isaac Brock (1769-1812). Originally from the Channel Islands, service takes him to the Netherlands, and to Copenhagen aboard Nelson's fleet. Brock is tall, mild mannered and kind. A long and at times frustrating posting in Canada gives him excellent local knowledge that will prove essential. Brock is in charge of the defences of Upper Canada, which are painfully inadequate to the task, and much is down to Brock on keeping up morale. A US force under General Hull invades and Brock readies a smaller force, largely Indian and Militia, to block them. Brock's aggressive resolve inspires Tecumseh and the counterattack begins. Astonishingly, the Americans surrender their army and Fort Detroit. Brock now dashes back and confronts US forces crossing the Niagara. The British garrison holds on as the Americans attempt a surprise crossing long enough for Brock and reinforcements to arrive, but at the Battle of Queenston Heights, the general - visible and at the fore - is shot and killed. By his actions and death, Brock becomes the Wolfe of Upper Canada.

The Niagara Peninsular continues to be fought over after the battle. If the Americans are hindered from seizing it in 1813, it's in part because of a heroine by the name of Laura Secord (1775-1868). Overhearing a conversation between American officers of a plan to surprise an outpost, Secord resolves to warn the garrison. She makes it by circuitous paths 20 miles cross country, and her alert means Indian allies are mobilised in time to harass the advancing Americans. The invaders end up surrendering on arrival. Don't expect to have her pointed to you during your visit, however, as she'll only become famous much later on in life.

A number of the American statesmen of this period you may already have met during earlier visits, but some find their careers reaching their apotheosis at this time. Take James Madison (1751-1836). You may encounter him as a key author of the Constitution, and he's also twice President. Madison is short and wiry (don't ask about his health - he always looks a bit peaky). Initially a leading Federalist, his friend Jefferson wins him round to his way of thinking on limiting the powers of the central state especially on money matters. If you're a clergyman, note that he is a prime mover in separating Church and State, so given he's quiet don't blunder on about that at length. Madison is also the president who begins the War of 1812 so if you are a serving officer of His Majesty, you may be stopping by to visit his house and eat his dinner without receiving a formal invite.

The story of Hamilton and Burr sounds like the plot from an unbelievable novel. Alexander Hamilton (1755-1804) was born in the West Indies. Post independence, he is a critical contributor to the political debate establishing a more centralised form of government, more in getting the agreement ratified and exploring its consequences than in the drafting. Subsequently, he serves as the country's first Secretary of the Treasury. Perhaps it would be prudent not to discuss his family, as his French mother was married to someone other than his father when he was born, and his father subsequently abandoned her. Hamilton proves to be clever and hard working and is sent to America for education. He subsequently serves in the revolutionary army. Tellingly though, after the war he defends New York Loyalists in the courts, in the process contributing towards the establishment of a judicial review system. He also refuses when in power to argue for his home state of New York to host the national capital, preferring instead to push for the economic agreement he was more interested in (the "dinner table bargain" of 1790). So Hamilton is an eminent soldier, lawyer, economist and politician, and a star of the Federalist movement.

Aaron Burr (1756-1836) meanwhile as a young man served in the failed march on Quebec at the outset of the Revolutionary War, and is said to have tried to rescue the body of his dead commander. He endures Valley Forge, becoming embroiled in some of the politics of that place, and subsequently retires from the military on the grounds of ill health. After becoming a lawyer, he shares a practice with Hamilton in New York.

The two men have different views on politics, but the divisions will run much deeper. Ironically, when in the 1799 presidential election Jefferson and Burr tie, Hamilton opts to support his political opponent Jefferson instead of his former associate - Burr had defeated Hamilton's father-in-law in running for Senate several years earlier, and relations had soured. So a rebuffed Burr is forced to console himself with the Vice Presidency instead. Four years later Hamilton is again involved in hindering Burr's electoral chances, this time as Burr unsuccessfully attempts to become Governor of New York. The final trigger comes from a remark made by Hamilton at a dinner party, escalated by published correspondence from Burr, for which both men refuse to apologise. So in July 1804, it's pistols at dawn and the most famous duel in American history. The arrangement is said to be that both men will deliberately miss. But Hamilton fires first and instead of firing into the ground (as is the convention to show this), fires into the air; Burr still has his shot and takes aim. Hamilton takes a pistol ball to the abdomen and dies a day later.

Burr's career is over; indeed for a while he is wanted for murder. It gets worse, with accusations of him in 1807 seeking to engineer a war with Spain, a bungled attempt to wrangle backing from Napoleon, and then getting captured by the Royal Navy in 1812. Such reputation as he may still have by now has vanished.

By contrast, the War makes the career of Andrew Jackson (1767-1845). A backwoods lawyer, mind what you say to him: he has killed a man in a brawl over a slight. In the War of 1812, for reasons we can't quite understand he ends up commanding the forces defending New Orleans. By the simple but prudent expediency of hunkering down behind solid defences with sufficient firepower to hand, he is able to repel the British assault, becoming as a result a national hero. We predict future ambitions in the White House. He's not the only one, treading in the path set by Tecumseh's nemesis William Harrison (1773-1841). Harrison's nickname of "Old Tip" comes from his victory at Tippecanoe. He's long had a reputation as an Indian fighter, and political involvement in governing the wild north west. As Governor of the Indian Territory, he's responsible for suppressing the tribes in war and establishing a harsh peace agreement afterwards, securing tens of millions of acres of territory. In 1813, Harrison's forces finally kill the Indian leader and his route to the White House will be secured. As it happens, Jackson and Harrison will be bitter political opponents. If you see the latter standing in the outdoors, offer him an umbrella: we have a bad feeling about how many weeks he'll last in office with his tendency to loiter notwithstanding the rain.

Not all interesting characters are into politics or war. Take the fascinating Johnny Appleseed (1774-1845). His real name, we're told, is John Chapman. He's a travelling farmer who enjoys planting apple trees as he goes. Some say he barters them for essentials and lives a frugal life. You can spot him by his peculiar look, bare footed and sack-wearing as he is.

Over the border, it would be a mistake to assume Canada has been denuded of personalities by the loss of the star colonies. We begin with two French Canadians. Charles-Michel d'Irumberry de Salaberry (1778-1829) has an unusual and long service in the British army, having enlisted aged 14. He's fought the French in the West Indies, been shipwrecked, became a personal friend of one of the King's sons (the future Duke of Kent, who introduces him to Freemasonry), served in Ireland, and was one of the multitude who came down with malaria in the disastrous Walcheren Campaign. That brings him back to Canada at a fortuitous time, just as Canada's defences are being put in order. Salaberry is put in charge of a new Light Infantry militia unit, the Voltigeurs Canadiens, and is in command of a key sector during the American invasion, which he repels through clever deployment of inferior resources at Châteauguay. He is a hard task master and a disciplinarian, amicable but occasionally hot headed. To the military figure we can add the politician. Louis-Joseph Papineau (1786-1871) is an up and coming politician, who also sees service in the war. Looking into our crystal ball, we predict he will be a major political figure in the years ahead, an opponent of gubernatorial rule, and an agitator perhaps even of French Canadian independence during a period of revolt. As such, that would make him the French Canadian counterpart of York/ Toronto Radical William Lyon Mackenzie (1795-1861). But we are getting a couple of decades ahead of ourselves.

Canada's wilds generate many heroes of exploration and masters of survival. Among these, we would suggest spending time learning from the likes of Sir Alexander Mackenzie (1764-1820). Mackenzie's name is remembered after his passing by geography itself. A Scot by birth whose father had joined a Loyalist regiment, his career takes him into the Montreal fur trade. Competition in the 1780s becomes fierce and Mackenzie is on the trading front line, setting up new posts and routes across the unexplored Canadian hinterland. His first voyage disproves a river route assumed to run towards the Pacific and leads him to the Arctic instead. His second corrects some major mistakes in cartography and takes him so far west that he is the first person north of Mexico to cross the continent from coast to coast. He's a persuasive leader in times of difficulty, persistent, and diplomatic with the new tribes of Indians encountered. In later years, he briefly enters provincial politics, before taking a troublingly young wife and retiring to Scotland. His break-through journeys are further developed by explorer-traders Simon Fraser (1776-1862) and David Thompson (1770-1857). By a slight twist of timing, Mackenzie's arrival on the west coast narrowly miss generating a symbolic encounter. He arrives there just six weeks after George Vancouver (1757-1798).

Interested in a less energetic route to the West Coast? Then Vancouver's expedition is the one without the canoes and carrying around all that dried meat. He served under James Cook during the latter's Second Voyage looking for the Southern Continent. On the Third Voyage, he's on board when Cook explores North West America in 1778, and thus Vancouver is one of the first Europeans to have landed on King George's Sound. Remaining questions about how Alaska fitted into the geography of the continent, and the prospect of lucrative pelt markets in China, encourage the Admiralty to send a new expedition a decade later. Vancouver maps the region which is contested with Spain, in passing establishing a fleeting protectorate over Hawaii. He is a remarkable surveyor, a competent commander who looks after the welfare of his men (though coming across as a bit superior), and his achievements are demonstrated by the proclivity of places named after him.

We mentioned earlier that North America is devoid of Lords. There is a peculiar exception in the north. Thomas Douglas (1771-1820) is the Earl of Selkirk. A generous, caring man, the future Earl as a boy is shaken by the raids of John Paul Jones, and later on by the realities of the Clearances. He decides to help the displaced Highlanders by supporting their emigration to a better life in Canada. After some passing successes in the east, he turns his attention to the west. This sets him in conflict with the fur traders. His huge Red River Colony, all 300,000 acres of it established from 1812 onwards, sits astride the main fur routes. Also unfortunately, the main body of settlers arrives after a poor harvest, meaning that the local Métis become angered at being banned from selling pemmican to passing traders as is their usual way of making an income. As of 1815, this has degenerated into an outright war, with the main fur trading company backing the insurgents. We think the broader dispute with the Métis isn't going to be settled any time soon, and can only speculate what will happen when it's confirmed that the American border runs through the middle of the land grant. Unfortunately, it's not doing much for the health of the Earl either.

As well as his lordship, you might also get a couple of brief glimpses of royalty, since members of the Royal Family are garrisoned here for a short while as part of their tours of duty. It means you'll find royalty here more often than you might even in Scotland. George III's son, Prince William (later William IV) is stationed here in 1786. His brother, Prince Edward, spends most of the 1790s here, and indeed from 1794 is in command at Halifax. His travels even take him through Boston at one point. Expect a stickler for parades at ungodly hours and a clampdown on drinking and gambling. On the positive side, the city is subject to some major improvements and building work. His mistress, Mme de Saint-Laurent, despite sharing the name of the river is not Canadian but French, which explains how the exiled Duc d'Orléans (future King Louis-Philippe) ends up making a social call on them. The two spend many happy years together. Sadly Edward, now Duke of Kent, is in later life obliged to set her aside and marry: the result will be a daughter called Victoria.

Chapter 7

Where to Visit

The History Route: Ten Key Early Colonies

Many of the towns you will encounter will generally be only three or four generations old. That will be especially true the further into the untamed hinterland you go, or the nearer to borders claimed by other colonial powers today or in times gone by. Colonising was a dangerous adventure when the Spanish were at their zenith and your reinforcements were several thousand miles away.

But there are towns with a much older pedigree. They might not pass for truly ancient foundations, but they lead a straight path back to the earliest days of the pioneers. Some are just ghosts of their former selves, haunted woods and ruins that people say are just the sites of vanished homes but where no evidence now remains.

The oldest colonial settlement is, as you might expect, Spanish. Along with the Portuguese they were the trailblazers of colonisation, and while the English weren't too far behind there was a bit of a gap from our ancestors' scouring the bitter northern seas in search of a western route to Cathay, and successfully planting lasting settlements in cold woods and subject to the good will of numerous Indians.

So if you are seeking the first footprints of history you should go to Florida. The city of St Augustine was founded in 1565 as a cornerstone of Spain's trade route, and as part of an attempt to elbow the French out of North America – it was put up just after a nearby Huguenot colony was ruthlessly obliterated. The English threat remained however, which accounts for the fact that the only building that predates 1702 (when our forces occupied and burned the town) is the fort that dates from thirty years earlier.

The Treaty of Paris leads to the city being ceded to Britain along with Florida. For the next twenty years it acts as a Loyalist stronghold, but in 1783 is handed back to Spain as a reward for Madrid's support for the separatists. The high point of the colony however is past, as it is no longer as strategically useful. However, we do recommend you visit as an accessible taster of Spanish New World Culture.

Our second colony involves a haunting mystery. Roanoake today is a jumble of trees, but it hides a lost settlement the legend of which would baffle a latterday Pizarro or Cortes. Sir Walter Raleigh himself - a name likely to stir the sinews of any Englishman - was behind the enterprise. In 1585, following on from a scouting expedition, he sent Sir Richard Grenville to establish a fortified post tucked away beyond prying Spanish eyes in a bay on the coast of what would later become North Carolina. Over a hundred colonists were dropped off, with Grenville promising to return the following year with more colonists and supplies. Delays in his reappearing, plus trouble with the Indians, encouraged the settlers to accept the offer of a passing Sir Francis Drake to head back home. A few men stayed behind to keep the territorial claim alive: these would never be seen again. A second colonial expedition followed in 1587. Relations with the Indians had not improved; a settler was killed on the shore.

Still, the makings of a colony were there. Iron tools were being made locally. Homes were being built. The first English subject born in the New World was born here, Virginia Dare. But the Indians were a real risk, and the governor was forced to leave his baby grand daughter and sail back home for help.

He couldn't get back until 1590. When he arrived, the settlement was deserted, and the only hint of what had happened was the word "Croatoan" - the name of an island, or a misspelling of an Indian tribe - carved on a post. As mysteries go, it's a long way from being solved.

Another "might-have-been settlement" is that of Popham. No doubt scholars will at some point reach a consensus on where it lies. But in 1607, along the northern wilds of Massachussetts, a hundred colonists tried to eke out a winter on a bleak, exposed shore. With food running out, half returned home. The rest endured a horrible time and sailed home the following year.

Had things turned out differently, Roanoake and Popham could

The church at Jamestown is one of the oldest brick structures in America, but has not been looked after recently.

have become thriving metropoles acting as gateways to the continent. If it is any consolation, the French had similar problems with their outposts in the wilderness. St Croix was founded by the admirable, albeit French, explorer Samuel de Champlain in 1604. The winter was dreadful, scurvy was rife, half the people died, the survivors went on to found Port Royal in 1605 instead. Somewhat happier was the founding of Québec in 1608 which turned into Champlain's second home.

Jamestown was also nearly a failure. It was settled in 1607, and its importance was that of a springboard for further settlement - nothing of the original site can be seen today above ground owing to fire damage from civil sedition in the seventeenth century: a church building from 1639 provides a rare visible relic but even this is just the fourth on the site, and from the mid 1700s it too will be abandoned and slowly decay. The first settlers provide a story that's almost entirely one of men enduring the bitter ravages of winter starvation; but we can't escape the legend of Captain Smith and Pocahontas. It's a story that will be familiar to readers: indeed, since she accompanied her later husband John Rolfe to England, you may even have seen her grave at St George's Church in Gravesend. The full story is a bit murkier than some of the fairy tales might portray and involves betrayals and murder - but that would be for a different book.

A location you've almost certainly never heard of is Cupids. It's up in Newfoundland as was founded in 1610. Properly speaking this was settling down in an already defined space because these shores were well known to seafarers, familiar as temporary stopping points for fishermen to land and to preserve their catch for the long journey home. Cupids upped the ante by creating a permanent local post, something that provided English fishermen (many from Bristol) with an advantage over potentially hostile competitors from the Bay of Biscay. Life here too was harsh, though in 1613 the first child was born. Once again, the colony failed, but it lasted long enough to act as a stepping stone for other enduring colonies and long enough for the company that was given the original rights to stay in business. Bristol's Hope, Renews, Ferryland and in particular St John's all emerged from this settlement as the colonists moved on.

A climate that they no doubt would occasionally have wished for could be found further south at what some style England's oldest surviving colony. St Georges at Bermuda was founded in 1612 and has been going ever since; a period of stagnation in the mid eighteenth century has been followed – thanks to the American Revolution and the need for a secure naval base – by an economic spurt. The island has latterly been developing a strongly military veneer with the construction of garrison buildings. The military presence and importance of the dockyards will remain, and a quick glance at its location on a globe easily reveals why.

But Bermuda is not the continental mainland. The first enduring settlement there was Plymouth colony, in 1620. At the water front can still be seen the first landing point, which is the original site of the celebrated Plymouth Rock, used as footing during disembarkation. The rock itself, a large rounded pale boulder, is under threat of being moved around town by sundry patriots. The town's also the location associated with the first Thanksgiving (see the section on this earlier in this book). Plymouth administratively was subsumed by Massachusetts, but in terms of its population not only survives as a direct link to the past on its original site in a way earlier colonies have failed to do, it has generated a series of offshoots that have spread across this area.

Piscataqua you most certainly will not have heard of, but in its way is just as important an early settlement. It was founded in 1623 in New Hampshire as a fishing community: its Indian name comes from the river it sits on, and it was also known at the time as Pannaway. The settlement never grew beyond a large farming estate, though presumably its presence encouraged other communities to settle in its vicinity shortly thereafter, particularly neighbouring Portsmouth.

By comparison, Boston (founded 1630) is now starting to look in this company a little arriviste. As you might by now have come to expect, the story is a little more complicated. North Weymouth along the coast was founded in 1622, and then initially abandoned. It was securely resettled in 1623, but in the interim one family ended up in the vicinity of what would later be settled as Boston.

But in any event, by the 1630s we are starting to see a more widespread branching of settlements and more enduring roots being put down. Obviously a number of dangers would still have existed for the original colonists, but their uniqueness from a tourist viewpoint starts to diminish as the rarety value diminishes and they become aspects of our contemporary history. So let's turn away from highlighting the New World's antiquities, many of which have in truth been lost to sight, and move instead to what treasures await the traveller today.

Canada

Geography, and a southerly gale, may make your first point of call Newfoundland. If you're familiar with the West Country, this will probably be a home from home (including the accent). The fisheries are facing a bad time in the early eighteenth century thanks to a drop in the catch, and a lot of people are emigrating. But markets do recover. After 1713, you may be surprised to still be encountering French fishermen who retain curing rights on the coast of the "Treaty Shore" for their catch, but it's the American fleet that grows in importance over the years and even becomes a negotiating issue after the Revolution.

If it's French flavour you're after, head west. Acadie is the site of Port Royal, later re-established as Annapolis. Visit before the deportations happen, and you'll find a colony of a few hundred souls centred on a small fort, Vauban-style earthworks, and a magazine. The bastions are named after the French royal family. Remember that the port sits on the Bay of Fundy which has an immense tidal range (the Indians say it's caused by the splashing of an immense whale). Culturally, this is probably a better bet than heading north and stopping over at Louisbourg. The problem here is that this is even more of a military outpost and you're most likely to be visiting Cape Breton if you've brought artillery with you. Its walls are of stone, 2½ miles long and up to thirty feet tall - at least until the British army conquers and keeps it. At its height during French rule, its position means that it's the third busiest port in

North America.

After the conquest, however, you won't find much left. Halifax swiftly absorbs its role, and in the case of some of its buildings (such as the home of Sir Richard Bulkeley), its physical fabric. This port becomes the key naval establishment and military base in the north east. Early immigrants are the German, Scottish and Irish. The Revolution introduces an ex-slave community. There's a significant New England population as well that causes occasional political difficulties. On top of that, there's also the Micmac and Acadian hinterland. A yet further dimension is the presence for four years from 1796 of 600 "Trelawny Maroons", or Jamaican rebels.

Clearly there's a lot of work to be done over the nineteenth century to make the town's buildings reflect its growing importance, but the initial log palisade scratch town of the 1750s is already gone by the 1770s. The town has some of Canada's oldest protestant churches, the continent's first lighthouse, and as of the early nineteenth century a respectable municipal building and an eminent Palladian clock tower overlooking the bay from the Citadel (this latter landmark, a parting gift from the Duke of Kent.)

Halifax is foggy and cold and wet, by and large. You should feel perfectly at home. If you're after a bargain, saunter down to the wharves during the War of 1812 to see what you can pick up on sale from one of the privateers operating from here. Stay, dine or relax in the evening at the Great Pontac tavern: it's a famous three storey building opened in 1769 that you'll find near the shore. This is a classy establishment rather than a dive, frequented by gentlemen of quality. We recommend the mutton pies, from meat you may find freshly butchered on the premises.

So much for Nova Scotia and Acadie. New France of course is home to Québec. You'll appreciate the fortifications whenever you arrive as they are pretty robust, though the mid-eighteenth century walls are in fact the third ones in place and later visitors will miss seeing the original outer earthworks. The Hôpital-Général is a medical establishment from the late seventeenth century catering for the sick. Maillou House dates from 1737 and belongs to a major masonry contractor: it's a good example of transplanted French architecture. Under British rule, you'll find the city gains an Anglican cathedral, and the establishment of a local bishop is a colonial innovation. Older church buildings worth a visit are the Catholic basilica, which is starting to get rebuilt as it's been destroyed along with much of the city during the Conquest; and the church of Notre Dame des Victoires, built in 1688 and commemorating two failed attempts to conquer the city. It too is currently being rebuilt so expect work in progress.

Continue up river to Montréal. For now it's still got its fortifications, though we're not sure how long the urban planners will stick with them if it grows as we expect. As it stands you are basically looking at a fortified town - the original town of Ville Marie - and a series of villages on the wider plain. After the Conquest, the town becomes economically more important and attracts a vibrant merchant community, largely Scottish, attracted in large part by the fur routes to the hinterland. If you want a flavour of the French architecture, head for St Sulpice Seminary, whose building work largely dates from 1684 but with a main neoclassical gateway from 1740. The Sulpicians used to have an important role here, having taken over from another order as the legal owners of the island. The quality of their buildings reflects their status.

Overlooking the town is the mountain which gives the town its name. Yes it sits on an island, but it's a huge one so don't expect to be able to stroll all the way around it, especially as there are native communities on it. That leaves a lot of room for the settlement to grow. It's still quite a small one by the Low Season, with perhaps a population of around 5,000, but that means it's kept its French character – for now, at least. No doubt future immigration from the British Isles will affect this, unless the Canadien population listens to the exhortations of their Catholic priests and expands at a phenomenal rate.

Montreal and Quebec are in Lower Canada, in the context of the flow of the huge St Lawrence River that sweeps past both. Upstream, the capital of the province of Upper Canada is the new town of York (Toronto). There are two reasons to avoid it. In the first place, it is little more than a newly-built village. Secondly, such buildings as it has get trashed by the invading Americans. Unless you have business with the governor or are dropping by on some relatives or a function, we would recommend not much more than overnighting.

The North West Hinterland

Still, if it's the wilds and frontiers you like, go for it. There are places even less genteel than York. Fort Pitt has been built up over 1759-1761 to control the Forks of the Ohio River. It's an impressive fortification, pentagonal with five thrusting bastions, built near to a smaller French fort it supersedes. The fort on construction almost immediately gets flooded, so bring waders. It then plays an important role in securing the ground during Pontiac's rebellion. Within a decade it loses its military relevance (in part because of repeated water damage) and becomes a trading post, though it briefly regains its significance as an establishment for the Continental Army during the Revolution. After that, it is destined mostly to get torn down. However, the neighbouring village of Pittsburgh, admirably sited for river trade, will continue to grow and some early industries are starting to be set up here.

Ticonderoga is the fort that sits at the bottom end of Lake Champlain, north of New York. Visit during the French years, which are brief, and you'll find it called Fort Carillon. It's rather more pokey than Fort Pitt, but strategically very important in commanding the north-south interior route. The view, as a result, is distracting. The large kitchen gardens ensure there are plenty of fresh vegetables so you won't starve. If impressive French forts are your thing, ie you are a spy, you have dozens of outposts across the continent to choose from. Many are wood and not too grandiose, but we recommend taking your covert sketching skills to visit nearby Fort St Frédéric with its massive, almost medieval style tower. It'll get torn down and replaced by the less striking (but still extensive) Fort Crown Point in the vicinity. Both show promise of becoming the focus for major population centres, but these cities never quite emerge. More enduring is Fort Niagara, which sits at the mouth of the river on Lake Ontario. The "French Castle" will survive changes of possession over the years. At first glance, the main building looks more like a manor house dropped from old France.

Not all sites worth seeing in the region are man-made. Niagara's not just a series of battlefields; it's also home to an important tourist site thanks to its Falls. There's a log cabin by the

Horseshoe Fall (to the south) that serves ale, to help break your journey. It's a meeting spot to encounter the occasional traveller who's on this continent because Napoleon is interrupting the usual Grand Tour on another. Happily there are no crowds to distract from the awe of these immense and powerful waters. Just be sure to have secure footing if you pace around close to the cliff edge.

New England and the Old East

The great cities of America are also the gateways to the continent. Boston has a reputation for civil disorder, but don't let that put you off from visiting. It's not just the fact that it's got paved streets that mark it out. The port is defined by its harbour to the south, but you may be surprised to find a large body of water also limiting your route to the north. This is the Mill Pond, a man made creek from the last century that was created to supply power for grinding corn.

Boston is distinguished by its many spires, because it's a town of churches, some even of stone. Not all attendees are saints: note that if supping at the Green Dragon, you should steer clear of political controversy as many radicals haunt that inn. The Bunch of Grapes is a more upmarket alternative - you'll find it near the Town House, where the governor is. The same area houses the press and some good bookstores. The waterfront area is home to the nautical manufactures and stores. The town is noted for its old Latin school, modelled after the Grammar School in Boston, Lincolnshire.

When in the area, drop by John Singleton Copley's farm to meet the eminent painter, and perhaps even commission yourself a portrait. Stay clear of the area south of the Common, as that's where the 'liberty tree' is (before it gets turned into kindling).

The port is sufficiently developed and of such standing that you can visit it at any time and find it of interest and merit. Neither the 1755 earth tremors nor even the terrible fire of 1760 (worse than that of 1711) should put you off.

A conflagration is something it shares with its counterpart New York, which also endures one in 1776. Casualties of that blaze include the important Trinity Church, given its charter by William III and now being rebuilt – this time without the loan of building tackle by famed pirate Captain Kidd! Take time off from the neighbouring Battle of Queenston Heights to see how it's progressing. A survivor of the fire by contrast is the key meeting point known as Fraunces Tavern, after the owner. It's of sufficient quality to be chosen as the venue for Washington's farewell dinner with his military staff.

The streets here are paved, though more like Boston's north side in being a little higgledy piggledy in plan. If the weather suits, take a stroll in the park known as Bowling Green. Should you want to admire the equestrian statue of George III, get here before the revolution when it gets melted down into bullets. If the temperature is pleasant enough you've probably arrived at the wrong time, as high society will be out of town at their country escapes. Still, there's always trade to be done. If by contrast you've arrived with the Fleet, see if you can spot some bubbles peculiarly rising from the waters beside your vessel. The rebels have devised a peculiar bulbous submersible that they use to try to attach an explosive to one of our warships. Happily, they overlook the difficulties of affixing anything to the copper bottoms.

Philadelphia is a growing town, sturdily built from brick. Stylistically it is less varied than other places, but makes up for this by being at the forefront in urban street lighting. You might properly consider it a centre of innovation. Since 1743, it's been the home of the American Philosophical Society. If you're a man of learning then this is a definite way stop. The town hosts America's first botanical garden, library, hospital, and theatre. You can also find goods not normally encountered being manufactured on this side of the Atlantic, from pianofortes to carpets. So even if the architecture bores you, the social life won't. A symbolic building is the town's colonial legislature, which develops a wider political significance following the Revolution: admire the giant clock fronting it. The house-like building being built next to it is intended for the US Supreme Court. The other new building with a balcony is where Congress will move to when it returns to the city. We're not convinced it's big enough.

You might prefer a bit of older charm. In that case, consider a trip to old Salem instead. Yes, it's famous for all that witchcraft side of things but the locals prefer to drop all that. Instead, admire the huge dark beam rough hewn houses that evoke the seventeenth century wilds. It's surprising to note that the town is expanding into one of the top five on the eastern seaboard, thanks not so much for its wartime role as a haunt of privateers but rather because of some remarkable trading connections with the Orient. We're pretty sure we saw a whaler putting in during our visit; perhaps that's the future too.

The South

We're not certain whether the new nation's capital is properly in the north or the south, but then that's part of the point of it. Washington is clearly absorbing a lot of effort to make this a worthy national heart. This is good news as it means there is sufficient to burn down in 1814 as payback for all those atrocities you've been hearing about. After joining in the chaos torching the shipyard, head for the White House (which is already white by the war, but will soon need some serious redecorating). There is a wide range of excellent souvenirs to be had as the entire building becomes a Presidential gift shop. While the portrait of Washington has been rescued by the fleeing residents, there are still plenty of furnishings, hats, clothes, jewellery boxes, furniture, bottles of wine and general paraphernalia for your hall back home, including door knobs. Warehouses also have stocks of rum and tobacco that can be lifted. Note that on humanitarian grounds, the Patent Office is the one government building that will be ordered left unharmed. Of course, you'll spare the private property, but the forthcoming storm (from which you had best take cover as it's a stinker) will not. It causes casualties but helps add to the destruction and allows cover for the army to withdraw.

Your military tourism will also take you to Baltimore, the United States' third largest city and an obvious target given all the privateers based there. It's a major centre for the tobacco trade and, in times of peace, a key hub in the Caribbean sugar market. From the vantage point of the besieging forces, watch the play of rockets and exploding shells sweeping across Fort McHenry after nightfall. The defences won't fall but they look pretty and inspire a national anthem. That gives you plenty of time to sit back and admire the sons-et-lumières over a dinner of Maryland blue crabs.

Virginia Dare was the first English child born in the Americas. Baptism, as shown here, is a notable social event.

As you are in the area, why not drop by another key Maryland harbour? Annapolis (not to be confused with Nova Scotia's town of the same name, Annapolis Royal, above) is a well-to-do genteel community that even during the Revolution when deporting its governor invites him back. If you are there for any time you might be invited to join the Hominy Club - be sure to respond to the invite, like all letters between members, in verse! The social seat of royal government is Calvert House, which remains unfinished; the striking new State House (with its cupola, currently looking like a madly coloured cake) briefly assumes national importance afterwards. Definitely accept dinner invitations if offered to the Hammond-Harwood House, or the opportunity for a stroll in the pleasant grounds of William Paca's lofty home (avoid discussing politics as a matter of courtesy). The harbour's a noted entry point for slavers so you may need a strong stomach if you intend to go down to the docks. We encountered an unfortunate by the name of Kunta Kinte there.

Virginia's settlements are just as established and developed. The old colonial capital is Williamsburg, a college town with the feel of a market town back home. The Capitol building hosts local government, but also occasional social functions including dances. You may find some of the representatives at Mr Charleton's coffeehouse nearby. You might also try the busy market square. The Brafferton is where William and Mary College educates Indians, though numbers have badly dropped of late. The main academic site is the stately Wren Building. You can also find a theatre, the first colonial asylum, and a rather lush gubernatorial manor complete with busy gardens, perched at the top end of an elongated green. The title of "Palace" is doing the Governor's residence too much of a compliment all the same.

The fortunes of the town ebb after the provincial capital retreats to (seemingly) less-exposed Richmond in 1780. This is supposedly named after the vista over the Thames, though given the broken waters of the James River that run past here, the person doing the naming must have had either an appalling memory or an extreme bout of homesickness. You'll be too busy torching the place to appreciate its merits. Perhaps a more leisurely stay may instead be profitably ventured at Alexandria. This sits on the West bank of the Potomac, a little downriver from the site of what will become Washington. An important port for shipping the local tobacco, it is also a pleasant town to walk around.

But it may be that you are more interested in people rather than locations. In this area, thanks to the number of eminent personalities who reside in these parts, you can do both. Near Alexandria is Mount Vernon, Washington's home, to which (given the number of visitors arriving in a given year) you may well receive a dinner invite. This was the original farmhouse of his father, gradually over time augmented and improved into something a little more stately - compared with your average colonial residence which might make do with a couple of rooms, it's huge. To our eyes it also suffers from the blunt colour scheme, though we do admire the faux-stone wooden tiling. The back has a massive set of pillars providing a colossal frontage, the piazza, overlooking the river – a useful haunt on a hot day. When indoors, don't expect him to actually get behind the harpsichord as while he's an avid dancer, he can't play.

Jefferson's estate lies at Monticello, and has a more Palladian or classical air. Perched on a peak, it enjoys fine views. Enter via the classical portico and occupy yourself while waiting for an audience with the displays of Americana in the entrance hall. If you get the offer, do investigate the Book Room and the significant library held here. Two wings, or 'dependencies', provide for kitchens and parking spaces for carriages.

The Lee Plantation at Stratford Hall is smaller than you might expect if used to England's grand houses, even a little pokey, but it provides the visitor with an opportunity to experience southern country life - if you can abide the slavery. Just about everything you need in daily life comes from the estate, and the surplus is exported from the busy wharves. Tobacco, which drains the soil, is becoming a crop of the past here and yet the profit remains such that the lifestyle exceeds that of your average country gentleman back home.

Rather off the beaten track you might explore a little and head for Snee Farm in South Carolina, home to the less well-known Founding Father, Charles Pinckney. The owner is well placed to give you some alternative views on the constitutional debate, as he wrote the only draft submission contributed by a single hand. With a delegate for every one thousand voters, we shudder to think how big the state buildings would have to be in a couple of hundred years had he won that argument, though a significant number of his other ideas did make it into the final draft. If he's away because of the war, you may yet bump into a couple of captured revolutionary generals housed on parole there.

Norfolk is very much a trading centre and a town of warehouses and naval goods. It's a prosperous port and transhipment centre, though will be very badly damaged by the events of 1775-6. You'll not find much left other than the sturdy Church of St Paul's.

Head further south and you move into territories that are far more lightly populated. Charles Town is the key urban centre of the South, indeed the fourth largest urban centre in the colonies, trading heavily in rice, cotton and indigo - and slaves. In terms of its population, it is largely a black town. Judging by the number of spires, it's also quite a god-fearing one. Much of it is made from wood, and it shares with Savannah the indignity of a poor sewerage system.

Unusually, you may find if you take lodgings, the garden area is portioned out amongst the building's residents. Eating out? Try the local oysters, fresh from the river.

Places you may get a chance to call upon are big and boxy Drayton Hall (a plantation also being used as military headquarters), and of course the Old Exchange where you'll do any merchant business that you're over for. If you enjoy good contacts in town, inquire whether you might be permitted a review of the holdings of the Library Society - a collection inspired by the creation of the British Museum, though whose founding collection sadly will be destroyed by fire.

Charles Town has another feature that's unique to England's colonial settlements - fortifications. What's of use to keeping the Spanish and Indians at bay also proves handy with another early eighteenth century peril in these parts - pirates. Some have a better reputation than others. Stede Bonnet, for example, is known as something of a gentleman. If you encounter him in women's clothing, note that he is not a normal cross dresser, just attempting to escape.

A Carolinas particularity which is worth a possible detour to experience can be found at the community at Harkers Island. We said earlier there were four main accents; the reality as you might expect is a little more complex, and here's a marvellous example. Along with the similarly remote Outer Banks islands off Virginia, the isolation of the local community has preserved something of the old West Country accent. Even putting aside how non-English native speakers in the conquered colonies pronounce things, we imagine accent diversity will grow as the territories develop and expand. Places such as these still show rare echoes of the originals, intermingled of course with peculiar locally-invented words.

Savannah was Georgia's first town, where for a while they say worship was free, while rum, slavery and lawyers were outlawed. That was before the Revolution though, and before the invention of the cotton gin - back when tobacco was king and the cotton estates hadn't been introduced in these parts. It's notable as being the original planned town with wide streets and urban parks, which should give you some assistance when finding a safe place to shelter during the major fire of 1796. The blaze will spare the popular Pirate's House - a tavern, and former home of the curator of the experimental garden. Ask for a beer from the Oglethorpe brewery. There's also the original Lutheran Church, or if you are more experimental in your worship, the First African Baptist Church.

Augusta's founding followed a couple of years after Savannah's. Named after the Princess of Wales, this hinterland site dominated trade with the interior and secured British control, though tensions involving the traders and Indians versus the settlers are driving many of the latter into the camp of the rebels.

The Spanish South

Remember that for much of this period, beyond Georgia the territory is part of the Spanish Empire. There are certain procedures you should follow to avoid being taken for a smuggler or invader.

Proper etiquette on arrival at a Spanish harbour is to fire your cannon three times, or if your ship has none, a musket. Try to remember not to put anything in the muzzle when you load, as this can cause embarrassment. Hopefully your ship carries a 'thunder mug': not a chamber pot, but a sawn-off cannon somewhat resembling a tankard that can often fulfil a signalling purpose.

Florida's key destination is Saint Augustine. Of course at its heart is an old star fort, the Castillo de San Marcos. Unfortunately, if you're after the old town that's your limit, as the rest got burned down by our forces in 1702. The town plan at least is original and the rebuilt settlement does still carry something of Iberian colonial charm – at least the bits that survive our major attack in 1740 too. Spain gets the colony back for a while in the end, but its heyday is past. Even the atmosphere is a bit different, thanks to an influx of Minorcans adding a little bit of a Catalan flavour that's rare in the New World. Extend your stay in these parts with a stop off at Pensacola, over in West Florida. If you prefer to slum it on the frontier, at least do it where the weather's nice. This is the outpost's outpost, whose development is hampered by Indian raids, occasional hurricanes, and a period of French occupation, but at least it's sunny. Under British rule it starts to flourish and becomes a colonial capital of sorts with plans for urban development. Loyalist during the Revolution, Spain captures it and keeps it in the peace conference. You'll find it becoming increasingly Americanised as the years go on.

The French South

If you're this far south you may as well continue a few extra miles. Drop in on Mobile which lies just to the west. This is the original French capital of these parts, before it was moved further away from the British. Naturally, it's centred on a fort. Take the opportunity to stock up on some of the local French faience ware for your kitchen back home. The real magnet, however, lies further along the coast.

New Orleans is the gem of the Gulf of Mexico. Get down to the heart of the place, the French Quarter, before the major fires of 1788 and 1794. By the time these happen, the place is in Spanish hands so that will change the feel of the town when rebuilding starts. Shortly afterwards, the province gets handed back to France and then sold on to America so the atmosphere further changes. This is particularly so in the business district where the newcomers tend to settle. Canal Street provides a buffer zone between the two communities. The waterfront has as you might expect more of a rough feel to it, whereas the Garden District is becoming distinctly upmarket.

It's a peculiar town, full of exiles from New World revolutions and uprisings, but also of strong Creole influences too. That includes the food. The town itself is compact and set out in easily-navigable grid form, but if you can't get in (because Andrew Jackson is stopping your regiment from advancing, for example), at least you can test out some of the tasty Cajun cuisine in one of the settlements lying about the broader Mississippi Delta.

The Wilder Wilderness

Perhaps the colonies are not your cup of tea. Perhaps the colonies won't let you have your cup of tea, and you want out. Either way, there are always the paths more seldom trod. The far north offers opportunities of advancement through the fur trade, if you are an intrepid and self-reliant soul. Hudson Bay, depending on your viewpoint, is a bleak savage landscape untouched by civilisation and far from the barest of comforts. For those who have mastered the crafts and skills of the outdoors, often at Indian

hands, those same hills and streams instead offer the bare essentials man needs to survive and even to thrive. You can find a number of trading outposts dotted around the end of the great expanse of the Bay, and peppered at stages inland. These take the form of low forts or block houses, developing into more settled communities over time. Examples of key posts you may want to experience can be found at Prince of Wales Fort, York Factory, and the key administrative centre of Moose Factory south of James Bay; while of interior outposts you'll find examples include such places as Kootenae House by the Columbia River, and across as far as you can get sits the disputed trading post at Nootka Sound. But you had better be good at handling isolation, and note that that there is an intense and bitter rivalry developing between the Hudson Bay Company and the North West Company as the latter tries to break into the former's established monopoly.

Or you can aim for the Indian cultures of the Great Lakes and the continental interior. In particular, we would suggest you head for the brief promise of the settlement of Tippecanoe. Prophetstown, as it's also known, is a Shawnee site that sets out a rather different model of how to build a community. Don't expect any music halls when you come to the Wabash River Valley. Of the site itself we've heard very little, so do let us know what you find once you get inside the palisade. The reports we've heard point to several thousand people in dome wigwams made from reeds, bark and canvas, plus a scattering of more familiar-looking log frontier buildings, all set out in a well laid-out pattern. Conical shelters called tepee, if you are offered one, are a tourist's treat, at least in warm weather for fans of outdoor camping. Chances are though that you won't find many as they are mostly seen further west, and perhaps you'll be directed to dine and sleep in a communal building intended for visitors. Free-standing flat roofs are either there to provide shelter, or as viewing platforms for monitoring the crops. You might also be able to use one to get a grandstand view of the horse and foot races the locals enjoy indulging in. When you have a wander – and you should always take care never to absent-mindedly offer offence as you do the rounds – keep an eye open for the Medicine Lodge and for the main community hall where official business is conducted by the town leaders, in particular the Prophet, and his brother. The Prophet himself is related to have unusual ideas and special powers, but more than that we cannot say.

Before you go

A well-prepared traveller can save himself a lot of effort by making use of his time in London and around the country while waiting for the season for passage. Those too infirm or fearful of travelling might alternatively see a little of America in their own back yard. Here's how.

We start with the colonial agents. Since the middle of the seventeenth century, these are the political and near-diplomatic representatives of the colonial governments in London, lobbying ministers and Parliamentarians on their behalf. Their workload will explode as the tax issues take centre stage, lobbying for relief just as the London merchants are finding themselves far less dependent upon the American market alone. Yet you may yet find a meeting with one of their number an insightful starting point from which to plan your itinerary. More to the point, you may request letters of introduction to key parties, though you may be advised not to lightly importune as - given the volume of traffic to America - the agent might be approached to sign scores of such notes in a year. Agents include such characters as Henry McCulloh (North Carolina), Charles Garth (South Carolina) and Dennys de Berdt (Massachussetts Bay). But by far the most illustrious is Ben Franklin, who has the added advantage unlike a number of his colleagues of actually being from the colonies. For some sixteen years he is living in London. You'll find him at 36, Craven Street in the heart of the capital. We thoroughly recommend a visit. Even after his departure, on the eve of the Revolution, the place still bears an echo of its former resident.

Or you might turn to speak with those with whom he is employed to lobby. A few minutes' walk away of course is the old Houses of Parliament. This ancient sprawl of mediaeval buildings may look like a fire risk to some, but it houses some of the greatest minds in the English speaking world (even if at times their understanding of the difference between the East Indies and the West Indies seemingly leaves a lot to be desired). It's here of course that the great political debates on the future of the American continent will take place, on taxes and on war, on the founding of cities and the inking of borders.

A trip to the bull pit of Westminster reminds us what the departing colonies are losing. Even with their medley of heroes, the new Congress offers in the main but pale reflections of the great men of the English Speaking world in this age.

Find a gallery spot for the House of Lords in April 1778 and you'll witness the swansong of Lord Chatham, or Pitt the Elder (after whom Fort Pitt is named). By now he's a bit doddery.

The speech itself, contrary to some recollections, concerns itself more with the need to batter the French; when he sits down, he's reminded that the subject of the debate is about the war in the colonies. As the next speaker progresses, he becomes more and more agitated, and then gets up to speak again. The effort is too much; as he collapses, his son (Pitt the Younger, who had been watching nearby) dashes over. He dies a month later. The emblematic moment is caught in Copley's famous painting.

In the Commons, the debates on America are moments for Charles James Fox to shine. If taxing the colonies provided opportunities for the Opposition to tear into the Government - and how much of this is genuine as opposed to opportunism, it's difficult to judge - the descent into rebellion allows them to tear it apart. Fox is amongst the most outspoken and coherent critics. The scale of his oratory is matched only by his girth, both of which make for a good dinner guest. It is perhaps telling of his style that he later pens a pamphlet called An Essay Upon Wind, attacking the Lord Chancellor (to whom it is dedicated as an eminent peteur, apparently). It's not as outrageous as it might appear, given that Jonathan Swift, author of Gulliver's Travels, some decades earlier pens a similar spoof. We understand he writes it for a bet.

Alternatively, speak with a colleague on a mission. Fox has been outspoken on one particular issue but realises a key campaign stands more chance of being successful with someone else in the lead. The work of William Wilberforce will have a profound effect on the colonies. Short, wiry, but charming, his campaign – the slow culmination of dogged work by many – will change the lives of millions for the better.

Of course, you may not know what the various people look like. Out of Season travellers may consider a trip to the National Gallery or to the National Portrait Gallery. Here you can see, face to face, James Cook, Thomas Paine, George Washington, William Wilberforce, and a striking portrait of a behatted George III. Loiter in particular for a while in front of the full length image of Sir Banastre Tarleton in his campaign uniform.

Not all politicians are in Westminster. You could learn about America by heading over to the Tower of London! Over 1780-1, Henry Laurens is held there having been captured off Newfoundland in transit. Though the buildings are far from luxuriant, he has access to top wines and champagne, befitting his status as a former President of the Congress and eminent rebel. He is released in exchange for the captured Lord Cornwallis. After becoming one of the Peace Commissioners, he'll retire from public life and withdraw to his South Carolina estate. A less happy status befalls other prisoners you might be able to encounter. If you are in Edinburgh, for example, you might go up to the Castle. The graffiti-etched vaults here hold a number of nationalities as the Rebellion turns into a world war. Amongst them are captured American privateers. The cramped conditions are somewhat better than they would be on board a prison hulk, and indeed with all the hammocks and small windows are even a little nautical in their feel, but leave a lot to be desired. That also means though you may be able to do a bit of a trade, exchanging luxury provisions like tobacco for some of the carved items like model ships the prisoners produce.

Elsewhere there are curious surprises. In Tottenham, the Church of All Hallows is an admirable and lofty remodelled mediaeval construction. But from 1801 onwards, listen when the bells peal and you can encounter the sound that Montcalm's men heard. The belfry houses a seventeenth century Flemish bell that used to be in Quebec before the Conquest. So when you hear the Service Bell strike G, you're listening to the same sound the Garrison heard when it was being summoned to the walls.

Perhaps taverns are more your haunt. The Shippe (much later: The Mayflower) lies on the Rotherhithe waypoint from which the Pilgrim Fathers departed. Looking out over the river, cast an eye at the gibbets. It's where pirates are exposed to the birds and to the rising tide. In 1701, you may spot the festering corpse of Captain William Kidd. If you didn't encounter him in New York, you can observe him now. But you can find out all about his career and world in our sister guide book, Shiver Me Timbers: A Pirate's Life for Me.

Still interested in some olde worlde sightseeing? Over in Borough, the Queen's Head tavern (much later: Queen's Head Yard) is where the Harvard family money comes from before John Harvard sells up and emigrates with his books. Out of town, head up to Boston on the east coast to continue the Mayflower connection. The old Guildhall there has the cells in which the Pilgrim fathers are said to have been held during their trial. If it's

Jamestown that fascinates you, take a seat in the drawing room at Knole House in Kent, and ponder over the settlement maps drawn up in that very room for the founding of Jamestown.

Sulgrave Manor in Northamptonshire dates back to Tudor times, though is largely now (with alterations and the expansion of the north wing) made up of the familiar local stone. It's the ancestral estate of the Washington family, and if you are observant you'll be able to spot in several places the family coat of arms: three red stars on a white background above two red bars. Perhaps it's just a coincidence, but it's strangely reminiscent of the new rebel flag...

Or you might be after more recent colonial connections outside of London. In which case, you might head for the house of Thomas Paine. His cottage is at 20 New Street, Sandwich, where he briefly works as an Excise official. It's not for long though, as after the death of his wife he moves. From 1768 til he emigrates in 1774, drop in on him on the High Street in Lewes under the shadow of the Norman castle. You might equally bump into him about town, or engaged in debate at the Headstrong Club (held at the White Hart Inn).

Fractious argument not your thing? Then direct your carriage to Westerham in Kent, and to the house called Spiers on the Maidstone Road. It's here that Brigadier Wolfe grew up. You might spot him having a farewell drink at the George and Dragon when he's on the off. On a later visit, you might come across another local resident, Pitt the Younger. Indeed, it's under an oak four miles away that Pitt, Wilberforce and future Prime Minister William Grenville resolve to introduce the Bill abolishing the slave trade.

Some venues provide a ruder insight into American politics. The Revolution can be felt even here, thanks to the depredations of John Paul Jones. Cautious, camouflaged or distant observers with a spy glass can monitor his progression at several stages. Whitehaven in 1778 sees a botched raid on Cumberland that could have crippled the nation's coal fleet. Off the coast of Yorkshire, the battle of Flamborough Head the following year might best be monitored (other than on the ships themselves: dangerous) from the mighty cliffs of Bridlington. It's a two hour engagement, so bring something to sit on and perhaps some luncheon. By contrast, we counsel staying clear of Lord Selkirk's estate on St Mary's Isle, near Kirkcudbright, as the Americans are on a plundering and kidnapping venture.

Many of His Majesty's regiments hold keepsakes of their time spent in the colonies. Royal Marine officers (RM Museum, Portsmouth) will show you Colonial colours they captured at Bunker Hill. The 54th (Rifles Museum, Dorchester) has mementoes relating to the late Major André, formerly of this regiment. The 38th Foot has a grenadier officer's mitre headgear (Staffordshire Regiment Museum, Lichfield), so has the North Lincolnshire Regiment, (Museum of Lincolnshire Life, Lincoln). The unit's battle honours include Lexington, Bunker Hill, Germantown, Monmoth and Rhode Island. Meanwhile the 85th Light Infantry (Shropshire Regimental Museum, Shrewsbury Castle) recalls their service over 1812-15.

Appendix 1

Pocket Timeline

Out of Season

Nothing happens in isolation. Here are the key events of early colonial history in North America. Dates for European wars are as they affect this continent: they may start or end earlier or later. This is a period of exploration, of bootstrap survival, vicious and pitiless fights with the natives, and a handful of rugged adventurers making and breaking claims to vast swathes of the New World.

Fifteenth century: *Grand Banks known?* West Country fishermen may conceivably know of the great fisheries and landing places for drying cod, but keep them a trade secret.

1496-1499: *English discoveries begin.* 1496 first voyage of Sebastian Cabot, Venetian expat in the service of Henry VII; turns back after crew and weather trouble. 1497, second voyage; he discovers what is called New found land (though the actual landfall is uncertain). 1498, third voyage. 1499, William Weston from Bristol follows.

1508-1509: *The next generation.* Sebastian Cabot continues and extends his father's work. Support drops away once Henry VIII becomes king. From 1512 Cabot Jnr is on the payroll of Spain but much later returns, exploring links with Muscovy.

1534-1542: *French arrive.* 1524-1525, Giovanni da Verrazano leads French scouting expedition along most of the east coast. 1534, First voyage of Jacques Cartier to Gulf of St Lawrence. 1535, second voyage as far as Montreal rapids. Overwinters and returns to France in 1536. 1541-1542 third voyage; on return, minerals found turn out to be worthless.

1576+: *Hunt for the North West Passage.* 1576-1578, Frobisher explores northern straits seeking the short route to China. Three voyages of discovery, but only worthless ore found. 1578-1583, Sir Humphrey Gilbert's attempts to explore and seek possible colony sites ends in the loss of Gilbert and many of his crew. 1585-1587, John Davis's three expeditions to seek the North West Passage. 1616, Bylot and Baffin in the Arctic: the suspicion grows the passage does not exist.

1579: *First English claims on the mainland.* Drake lands and claims part of North America for England. He calls it New Albion. Others will know it as California.

1584-1590: *Roanoake.* Colony founded and abandoned; then refounded and settlers disappear.

1607-1611: *Voyages of Henry Hudson.* 1607, explores area around Greenland. 1608 off far north of Russia. 1609, with Dutch crew explores Nova Scotia and New England. Clashes with natives in New York area. Discovers the Hudson River. On his return journey his vessel is impounded. His final voyage in 1610 is under an English flag. He enters the Hudson Bay but is trapped by ice. 1611, the crew mutinies and he is cast adrift, presumably dying shortly thereafter.

1607-1622: *Faltering settlement of Jamestown.* A third of colonists dead within the year. The Starving Time: 1609, diet of rats, shoe leather, and cannibalism. Disputes with local Powhatans escalate and generate brutal reprisals. Pocahontas captured and acts as a go-between: 1614 cease fire. 1622, Indian massacre kills a third of the colony; Jamestown itself is forewarned but many smaller communities are destroyed. Colonist response is not to sail away and the fight back over the next ten years (Second Anglo-Powhatan War) is brutal. It starts in 1623 by poisoning 200 Indian warriors at a peace conference.

1603-1627: *French colonial settlement begins.* 1603, Du Pont expedition along St Lawrence. 1604, St Croix settlement founded by Du Gua de Monts, but fails. 1605, explores coast of (future) northern New England. 1608, founding of Québec. Local coup plot fails. 1615-1616, Samuel de Champlain's expedition into the interior. 1627, Champlain put in charge of the Québec colony.

1613-1632: *French loss of Acadie.* 1605, Port-Royal founded. 1613, expedition from Virginia destroys it. 1614, Port-Royal re-established upriver. 1621, part of the royal cession of land on establishment of the Scottish baronetcies of Nova Scotia. 1632, Acadia restored to France.

1629-1632: *An English Quebec.* 1627 Britain and France at war. 1628 English ships arrive at the St Lawrence and start to capture settlements. They are led by the Kirke brothers (half-French Huguenot and originally from Dieppe). They intercept shipping, food supplies and reinforcements. On returning in 1629 Québec capitulates. Technically, however, its conquest has taken place after war had halted in Europe so French settlements are handed back as part of the peace treaty in 1632. Champlain restored but dies in 1637.

1620-1640: *Exodus and colonisation.* Religious exiles arrive in North America in numbers, driving a key spate of enduring colonial settlements.

1626+: *Other competitors.* 1626, first Dutch concessions. 1638, first Swedish settlement under Peter Minuit. 1643-1645, Kieft's War (Dutch vs Wappinger Indians). 1655, Dutch take Swedish territories. Sweden's Indian allies begin Peach War, following a colonist killing an Indian woman for taking a peach from a tree. 1658+ war with the Esopus Indians. 1664, Dutch lose territories to British.

1634: ***Black Robe.*** Jesuits take over from Recollets in missionary work amongst the Hurons.

1634-1638: ***Pequot War. English traders mistakenly get caught up in an Indian dispute with the Dutch, and inter-Indian rivalry.*** Mystic Massacre: militia destroy a village. Pequot flee. Treaty of Hartford divides their territory and the prisoners between colonists and Indian allies.

1642-1659: ***Troubles at home.*** English Civil War, Commonwealth, Protectorate, moves to a Restoration; religious upheaval.

1644-1646: ***"The Plundering Time"***: Third Anglo-Powhatan War. 1644, Indians massacre settlers. Triggers major mobilisation of the colonists, building of key forts, and offensives that break up the Indian confederacy. Virginia secured.

1650: *Treaty of Hartford.* Controversially-sited fort of Hartford triggers negotiations. Local deal between colonial governors fixes Anglo-Dutch borders.

1653: *First Anglo-Dutch war spreads to the New World.* 1651, Navigation Act bans foreigners from British colonial trade. 1652, outbreak of war. 1653, Hartford captured from Dutch. 1654, war concluded by Treaty of Westminster.

1654-1670: ***Acadia English again.*** 1636, Acadie riven by power struggles. 1654, Cromwellian troops are sent to support colonial militia under General Sedgwick against New Amsterdam. A local ceasefire however is in play, but noting French military support for the Dutch in the Caribbean he takes his men to capture Port-Royal instead. The action is controversial as war has not been declared, but wins official approval.

1660: *Dollard des Ormeaux.* French/Huron attempt to ambush Iroquois ends badly at (b) Long Sault. Perhaps the fight does protect Ville Marie from assault. Dollard and his dead companions enter French Canadian mythology.

1664-1667: ***New Anglo-Dutch conflict spreads to the New World.*** 1663, new Navigation Act toughens enforcement. 1664, war considered possible or likely. As tensions escalate over Africa, a force is sent to New England as reinforcements. Its commander arrives at New Amsterdam and demands its surrender, exceeding his orders but in keeping with escalations by both sides elsewhere. The settlement becomes New York. The Second Anglo-Dutch War breaks out shortly afterwards. 1667, Treaty of Breda. New York confirmed as British, French to regain Acadie but limits not defined.

1670: *American Treaty.* Treaty in Madrid limits English settler expansion southwards from Carolina. This fails in practice (Savannah for instance will be built on the wrong side of the line).

1675-1676: ***King Philip's War.*** Indian chief 'Philip' (Metacomet) attacks outlying encroaching Massachusetts settlements. Fighting escalates. 1676, (b) Bloody Brook: colonial militia defeated. Various towns evacuated or burned. Great Swamp Fight: Narragansett tribe defeated but pushed fully into Metacomet's camp. Pierce's company ambushed and killed. Providence burned, Rhode Island largely evacuated. But Indian tribes defeated in turn and Metacomet killed. Result: twelve towns destroyed but resettled; colonists appreciated they had saved themselves without support from home; Indian power broken in New England.

1676: ***Bacon's Rebellion.*** Economic difficulties, personality clashes, poor growing weather and clashes with Indians raise temperatures in Virginia. The hot-headed Nathaniel Bacon, cousin of Governor Berkeley, rebels against authority. Bacon assumes control, rampages amongst the Indians (many of them the wrong ones), and issues a justifying "Declaration of the People" - one hundred years in advance of a certain other one. Losing control again, he burns Jamestown and dies of the flux. Not really an early revolution, more a personal power struggle.

1682: ***Louisiana.*** La Salle arrives at the mouth of what would later be the Mississippi, but for now is the Colbert River, and claims the area for France.

1686: ***Doomed Deal.*** 1684-1686, rival British and French fur traders capture each others' ports and shipping in a private war. 1686, James II/VII and Louis XIV sign Treaty of Whitehall or Treaty of Peace. Colonies to be treated as neutral in any war that might happen between the two powers, thus securing trade, permitting continuing fishing, and discouraging the Indians. It also removes privateering, enforces the monopolies of the other state, and provides for support to the shipwrecked. But James is overthrown in the Glorious Revolution so fighting does spread. Fisheries clauses considered by British legal experts still in force when reviewed in 1753: they form the basis of treaty obligations ever since.

1686-1687: ***Incursion of direct royal authority.*** James II/VII introduces measures to coalesce colonies under direct royal control, with very limited right of representation and direct taxation. He is meanwhile overthrown and the policy ends.

1689: ***Lachine Massacre.*** Iroquois raid a settlement near Ville-Marie.

1689-1697: ***King William's War (War of the Grand Alliance/ Augsburg League).*** 1684-1689, ongoing Iroquois attacks and punishment counter-raids by the French culminate in massacre of settlers at Lachine. This exacerbates anti-British feeling. 1690, pro-French Indians attack New York settlements. Admiral Phips and Massachusetts militias bombard Québec ineffectually but fail to take it, unaware of food shortages within. Fighting continues but is limited to border raids, most notably 1692 the York Massacre in Massachusetts.

1692-1693: ***Salem Witch Trials.*** Nearly 200 people accused of witchcraft, 20 executed. 1697, day of fasting ordered in recognition of excesses. 1702, trials judged unlawful. 1711, compensation awarded.

High Season 1700 - 1763

Colonies have been planted and the game is now in play for a continent. World wars will be breaking out, with the continent playing the part sometimes of the trigger, sometimes as the bartering chips and spoils of victory.

Period **Events**

1701: ***Indian Treaties.*** 70 years of inter-Indian warfare (the Beaver Wars, over fur trading with Europeans) conclude with a huge conference and the Great Peace of Montréal. Meanwhile the Nanfan Treaty between the Five Nations and British asserts UK sovereignty over much of the mid West. Interior opened up to trade.

1701: ***Footprint on the hinterland.*** Antoine de la Mothe Cadillac establishes a fort at Détroit.

1702-1713: ***Queen Anne's War (War of the Spanish Succession).*** 1702, privateering and raids by French and allied Indians begin. Spanish attack but fail to take Charleston; Carolina militias take and burn St Augustine but fail to take the fort and withdraw. Spanish Indian allies subsequently crushed. 1703 raiding in the north escalates: 1704 Deerfield massacre. 1707, failed attack launched from New England on Port-Royal, Acadie. 1710, new attack on Port-Royal takes the city: renamed Annapolis Royal. 1711, Sir Hovenden Walker's expedition loses several ships and a thousand lives from mis-navigating up the St Lawrence river: attack on Québec is aborted. 1713, Treaty of Utrecht: Britain is ceded Newfoundland, Hudson Bay, and Nova Scotia. France retains Québec plus Cape Breton island, on which it develops the fortress of Louisbourg. Local French colonists, the Acadiens, largely stay under new British rule, swearing an oath of neutrality.

1710: ***Iroquois chiefs visit England.*** Four leaders from the Five Nations confederacy arrive in London to seek military assistance during a royal audience. They famously sit for portraits.

1711-1713: ***Carolinas.*** Encroachments lead to Tuscarora Indian War in North Carolina. 1712, Carolinas divided into North and South.

1718: ***Pirates of the Caribbean.*** 1713 Edward Teach begins his pirating career ("Blackbeard"). 1718, menaces Charleston which bribes him to leave. Ditches his pirate associates and runs off with the loot. Accepts an amnesty from the Governor of North Carolina, providing political cover in return for some of the spoils from his continuing career. The Governor of Virginia takes issue; Teach is killed in a battle with the Royal Navy at Ocracoke. Marks the beginning of the end of the high period of piracy.

1722-1725: ***Father Rale's War.*** British have difficulty explaining to the Abenaki Indians Nova Scotia has been transferred to their control. Jesuit missionary Sebastien Rale and the colonial governor at Quebec, Vaudreuil, say they should not confute sovereignty and possession, and encourage the Indians to resist British settlement. Raids and very widespread skirmishes follow. An expedition kills Rale and confirms British possession.

1727-1729: *Anglo-Spanish war.* Some actions in the Caribbean.

1739-1742: *War of Jenkins' Ear.* Tensions escalate after Spain is accused of abusing customs right to board and check British trading vessels. Named after a merchant captain said to have displayed the accoutrement the Spanish had cut off. 1739 British take Panama (whence Rule, Britannia!) 1740: Georgians fail to take St Augustine. 1741, massive British offensive against Cuba fails dismally and leads to the fall of Walpole. July 1742: major Spanish invasion of Georgia. (B) Gully Hole Creek followed by (b) Bloody Marsh: two minor skirmishes break Spanish morale and end their offensive. 1742 War of Austrian Succession breaks out in continental Europe.

1744-1748: *King George's War (War of Austrian Succession).* 1744 Britain at war with France. French capture Canso in Nova Scotia. Annapolis Royal held though. 1745, expedition from New England takes Louisbourg. 1746 French expedition to retake it fails. 1748, Treaty of Aix-la-Chapelle; Louisbourg returned to the French, which provokes outrage in the colonies.

1749-1755: *Father Le Loutre's War.* 1749, foundation of Halifax. French missionary Jean-Louis Le Loutre leads resistance by Acadiens and Micmac Indians against British settlement in conquered Nova Scotia. Le Loutre, the Micmacs, and the Acadiens under Joseph Broussard gain increasingly obvious levels of French support. However as war officially breaks out in the west, British forces are sent to take their key supply base at Fort Beauséjour. Le Loutre is himself captured. This secures British possessions in the area of New Brunswick.

1755-1762: *The Deportation of the Acadians (le Grand Dérangement).* Anticipating further war with France, Britain settles Nova Scotia to secure the new frontier. Acadien oath of neutrality replaced by required oath of allegiance. They hesitantly accept but, as they form a significant potential third column, expulsions begin. Perhaps 10,000 of the 12,000 Acadiens are expelled (reminiscent of the Highland Clearances). Some successfully hide out. 1763, after French colonial empire broken, military threat ends and oath accepted. Perhaps a third of deportees return but are forced to recolonise new territory especially eastern New Brunswick. Elsewhere, heritage survives in Louisiana (Acadiens>Cajuns).

1754-1763: *Death in the Forest: French and Indian War (Seven Years' War) begins badly.* Colonists start moving across Allegheny Mountains into French-claimed territories. 1754, British build a fort to protect their western interests. Workmen are driven away and the French start building their own, Fort Duquesne. Lt Col George Washington is in charge of a road building detachment. (B) Jumonville Glen: small French detachment ambushed. Washington retreats to hastily (and unfortunately, badly) construct Fort Necessity. Reinforcements arrive. They are besieged by the French. Occupants forced to surrender: Washington required to accept guilt for the murder by an Indian of a French officer on a diplomatic mission. 1755, General Braddock's military expedition lumbers forward towards Fort Duquesne. Approaching the fort, the advanced guard is ambushed; falling back the main British force is enveloped by confusion and after a three hour fight, Braddock is mortally wounded. The British retreat pursued by scalping Indians. Thus ends (b) Monongahela. Honour is restored further north. Sir William Johnson advances to take Fort St Frédéric on Lake Champlain, but finds a strong blocking force. He withdraws, but discovers he is being followed. He sends a force to investigate. These troops are badly mauled in an ambush at (b) Lake George. They retreat in a rush to the main force, who have put together hasty defences. The French attack but are in turn mauled. A second French force is also ambushed shortly afterwards. The result secures the Hudson Valley for the British. It also shows how terrible fighting in a forest is.

1754: ***Albany Congress.*** Colonial representatives and Indian allies meet. Iroquois not quite won over. Proposal by Benjamin Franklin for increased integration of the colonies generates agreement but no action.

1755-57: ***A war of strategy.*** 1755, a successful British siege of Fort Beauséjour (which the French had built to threaten Nova Scotia) cuts Québec from the seaboard. French raids on supply lines to Fort Oswego isolate it and force its surrender. 1757, new British outpost, Fort William Henry, is besieged. The garrison commander, Munro, is given terms and marches out – but the Indians attack many wounded and departing occupants including civilians (notwithstanding the presence or otherwise of any passing Mohecans). The fort is destroyed. Meanwhile, war escalates massively in continental Europe.

1758: ***Focus on colonial conquest.*** Three pronged attack planned in North America under new leadership. Major reinforcements sent while French are constrained by a naval blockade. 1758, Abercrombie unwisely attempts to storm Fort Carillon. At (b) Carillon he is bloodily repulsed by the French leader, Montcalm, after an ineffectual and piecemeal assault. But on the other fronts the British have greater success. Amherst besieges and takes Louisbourg (again). Forbes repeats the attempt on Fort Duquesne; his advanced guard is battered but the disaster this time is contained. The fort is evacuated and destroyed by the French. The site of Duquesne is finally taken, and Fort Pitt established in its place. Meanwhile, fighting has expanded globally, and will stretch from the Philippines, to Cuba, India and West Africa.

1759-62: ***A knockout blow.*** 1759, (b) Fort Niagara: French attempt to lift the siege ends in a bad defeat for the relief force. The fort is forced to surrender, resulting in the French evacuation of all the Ohio territory.

British push on Fort Carillon with overwhelming force leads to a French withdrawal. The British rename it Fort Ticonderoga. Wolfe descends upon Québec. His force launches a surprise crossing leading to (b) Plains of Abraham: Wolfe and Montcalm are both killed, Québec falls but is much ruined. The winter proves horrifying for garrison and civilians alike. The French lay siege, and successfully repel a foray at (b) Sainte-Foy, but despite the serious defeat, British reinforcements and provisions arrive in 1760. The siege is lifted and the balance again tips. Amherst takes Montréal, and French opposition in the north east of continental America ends. Accession of George III. 1761, Pitt the Elder resigns as Prime Minister on failing to push for pre-emptive war with Spain. 1762, French surprise attack captures St Johns, Newfoundland. It is recaptured three months later.

1763: *Treaty of Paris.* Under the terms of the final peace treaty, the British gain Canada and all lands east of the Mississippi except for New Orleans. French settlers at conquered Louisbourg deported. Some Caribbean islands, and two small islands off Newfoundland, are returned, but the French empire is broken. The Labrador coast is transferred to Newfoundland. Spain also hands over Florida in return for conquered Cuba. But Britain is even more heavily in debt – up from an incredible £72 million now to a preposterous £130 million. As context, less the interest, the Townshend taxes proposed below would have taken 3250 years to pay this off, even if fully collected.

Mid Season 1763-1783

Travel to North America in this period provides visitors with a glimpse of a brief Indian Summer of the British Empire there, a high point of hopes and aspirations, but also an increasingly polarised society.

Period Events

1763-1766: *Pontiac's War.* British administrative policy is seen as less favourable than France's to the latter's former Indian allies. Leader of the Ottawa Indians, Pontiac, heads an anti-British confederacy amongst Great Lakes tribes. Several forts and settlements destroyed. Paxton Boys: Pennsylvanian vigilantes murder innocent assimilated Indians. Expected French aid does not come to Pontiac but British expeditions do. War ends effectively in a ceasefire.

1763: *Proclamation on settlement.* British government swiftly moves to calm Indian fears by issuing a limit to settler expansion, seated at the head of rivers flowing into the Atlantic (thus excluding the Ohio and Mississippi basins). The Proclamation Line dividing colonial and Indian territories is to be garrisoned at colonial expense. A sensible and equitable arrangement is thus taken doubly badly by the colonies. Royal colonies of Quebec, East Florida and West Florida established.

1764-1771: ***War of the Regulation.*** Opposition in western North Carolina to corrupt local practices leads to violence. 1771, Regulators and Governor clash in a large scale skirmish: (b) Alamance ends the opposition.

1764: ***Sugar Act (The American Revenue Act).*** Intended as support for rum production, notably in Boston; taxes dropped on molasses imported from the West Indies, increased on foreign wine. Lumber, iron and other goods more strongly regulated. Reduced smuggling but hits the colonial economy which had been able to tap cheaper imports. Local vineyards encouraged. *Currency Act.* Uncertain local bank notes are replaced by a centralised system linked to Sterling, but too rigid; and customs issues also now policed by a British court, based in Halifax, applying a presumption of guilt.

1765: ***Stamp Act.*** Tax on paper, such as for legal documents covering everything from wills, university degree certificates, documents authorising privateering, appointments, liquor licences, land warrants, contracts, apprenticeship documents, playing cards (at 1/-), dice (despite their fabric, each pair at a lofty 10/-), pamphlets, newspapers, individual adverts within newspapers, and calendars (double if printed on both sides!). Alienates top strata of society. Riot in New York. *Quartering Act.* Colonies to arrange military accommodation. Soldiers may be garrisoned in private homes by compulsion - but explicitly only if no public accommodation such as inns is sufficiently available; persons aggrieved may appeal to civil powers, and abuse of the requirement can lead to an officer being cashiered. 1767, *New York Restraining Act*: New York Governor to withhold signing off laws until compliance. In Boston, soldiers set up camp on the Common to comply with the law while being near the city.

1766: ***Stamp Act Congress.*** Delegates from nine colonies meet together in New York to oppose the Stamp Act. They declare it unconstitutional as not voted through by them. The Act is subsequently repealed by Parliament, though accompanied by the *Declaratory Act* (American Colonies Act) which asserts the British Parliament to be the supreme authority over colonial assemblies in all matters, meaning particularly that it can levy taxes.

1763-1767: ***Mason-Dixon Line.*** Charles Mason and Jeremiah Dixon are brought in to survey the boundary southern Pennsylvania and northern Maryland. It will become a psychological boundary between the northern and southern settlements.

1767: ***Townshend Revenue Acts.*** Huge British state debts painfully apparent. Colonial taxes re-established on paper, tea, oil, paint, glass and lead. 1768, Boston trouble. Customs officials are forced to flee. Troops restore order, but are increasingly subject to provocations as tensions grow. Perceived high taxes and low money supply trigger decision by Boston merchants to not order in a range of goods from Britain, indefinitely so with regard to taxed items.

1770: ***General Repeal.*** Revenue from taxes had been dwarfed by costs of policing them, especially from keeping order in Massachusetts. Townshend Duties are repealed except tea only, on the same day as the...

1770 ...Boston "Massacre". Actually at the time it is just called the Incident on King Street. A sentry guarding a court house is taunted by some youngsters, and the soldier strikes one. A crowd forms and more soldiers are called out. The mob noisily encourages them to open fire. They open fire, contrary to their actual (drowned out) orders. Five people killed, several wounded. Radical lawyers defend the soldiers in court, two of whom are eventually convicted on a lesser offence. These cases are an early example of "reasonable doubt", a late example of "benefit by clergy" (ie special mediaeval church immunities, used to avoid the death sentence here), and a rare example of hearsay evidence introduced as a deathbed statement. The event was exploited - and the events too occasionally misrepresented - by radical propagandists.

1770: ***War Scare.*** Britain and Spain in conflict over the Falklands. The French draw back from escalating this to war at this stage given comparative naval strengths.

1770s: ***Radicals form groups.*** Committees of Correspondence formed to distribute propaganda. Groups of Sons and Daughters of Liberty set up as secret clubs. The most energetic and angry participants will be selected as delegates to Congresses. Responsible for tarring and feathering, and hanging effigies from Liberty Trees.

1771: ***Somerset case.*** Confirms an assumption that slavery is illegal in England.

1772: ***HMS Gaspee Affair.*** Rhode Island has been a centre for smuggling and wartime trade with the enemy. Unpopular customs ship lured to ground itself. Ship assaulted, crew seized, captain shot and wounded, and vessel burned (not the first). Rather than prosecute the brazen attackers, the local courts try to prosecute the commander. British Government tries to establish an outside court of inquiry (which is portrayed by local propagandists as a conspiracy).

1772: ***Pine Tree Riot.*** Illegal log cutters assault officials and mutilate their horses.

1772-1774: ***Hutchinson Affair.*** 1772, Franklin, in London, receives anonymously a batch of letters written by the royal governor of Massachusetts asking for more troops. He shows them to associates. 1773, they leak to the Boston press. Hutchinson leaves the city in a hurry. Franklin admits he is the source. His reputation in London as an official representative is dented and he leaves in 1774.

1773: *Tea Act*. East India Company in financial crisis with a large supply of unsold tea. British Government decides to sell it at discount in America. Misinterpreted as an attempt to buy support for the tax and deliberately ruin local importers. Tea largely returned or wasted but in Boston it becomes a political focal point. Further exacerbated by suggestions of a clamp down by the Governor of Massachusetts. Boston Tea Party. Locals disguised as Mohawks vandalise £9,000 of perfectly drinkable beverage. 1774, Burning of the Peggy Stewart. Annapolis tea merchant is forced to burn his own ship for fear of his family's lives.

1774: *Grasping the nettle:* the Coercive or 'Intolerable' Acts target Massachusetts. Boston Port Act. Suspension of loading and unloading of cargo in the port. Administration of Justice Act. Court cases relating to the disorder transferred to other jurisdictions, with compensation for travel, in order to protect officers of the court and jurors. Massachusetts Government Act. Colonial charter suspended locally and direct rule imposed. Quartering Act. Marginally extends billeting rights, by including access to barns, outhouses and uninhabited buildings. Quebec Act. French Canadian loyalties secured by authorisation of Catholic Church, association of old French west Mississippi territories, full legal rights, establishment of a provincial council. Arms controls. Ban on export of arms and gunpowder to the colonies. Munitions stocks to be more closely guarded.

Revere's false alarm. Paul Revere rides to Portsmouth, New Hampshire, with a rumour of British troops being sent to Fort William and Mary. A mob of locals attack the fort and seize munitions. The rumour turns out to be false.

1774: *Galloway's Plan.* Joseph Galloway, a Pennsylvanian delegate to the First Continental Congress now in session, creates an elegant and ambitious compromise. Each colony would remain self-regulating as before, but a Grand Council elected every three years would act as a continental Parliament, with a Speaker, a President General appointed by the King with right of veto and application, and covering issues affecting more than just the one colony including civil and criminal issues. United with, but inferior and distinct to, Parliament, both could veto the decisions of the other. War bills could be passed without waiting for Parliamentary assent. 22 October, rejected by six votes to five as news of the (Boston) Suffolk Resolves arrives, escalating the trade war by closing the local courts. Thus one vote changes history disastrously.

1774-1775: *Trade war erupts.* Continental Association: ban on trade agreed by the First Continental Congress. 1775, Parliament determines Massachusetts to be in a state of rebellion. Ban on New England fishermen operating in Newfoundland waters. New England Restraining Act. Colonial boycott of British goods thus countered by

British banning colonial trade with other countries.

1774-5: ***Last chances.*** Moves in British Parliament by Pitt the Elder and others to de-escalate are blocked. Earl of Effingham and others resign their military commissions as war looms. Conciliatory Resolution from Lord North: Colonies would support defence but only pay tax for managing commerce: with travel time lapse, rejected as fighting has by now begun. Second Continental Congress. Olive Branch Petition. Aug 1775, Peace party in Congress succeeds in getting agreement on a document expressing loyalty and seeking redress, but this is rejected owing to contrary messages also being pushed by the war party (such as the Declaration of the Causes and Necessity of Taking Up Arms).

1775: ***A Tragic Trigger.*** 19 Apr, Gage sends troops to seize militia munitions. Word gets out ("Ride of Paul Revere") and militiamen are mobilised and form up on Lexington Green which is en route. First known shot is an isolated militiaman whose powder charge does not actually ignite. Militia form up. (b) Lexington. Someone fires and fighting begins. Militia driven away. British march on to Concord, which they search for arms in a polite and restrained manner. An accidental fire is fought by soldiers and townsfolk, but the smoke is mistaken by militia watching outside of town as deliberate. They descend and encounter the bridge guard which sets about dismantling it, but again someone fires and (b) Concord begins. On withdrawing to Boston, the regulars find themselves under skirmish conditions and nearly break and run, rescued by a relief column. Significant British casualties: a couple of soldiers are subsequently reported scalped, and wounded killed. Militias mobilise centred on Massachusetts.

1775: ***Outbreak of War.*** Rebels swiftly surprise and seize Fort Ticonderoga with its munitions stockpile and cannons. 16 Jun, rebels entrench on Bunker Hill overlooking Boston harbour; following day, British assault the positions head on. Pyrrhic victory follows. August, Proclamation of Rebellion issued; rebels officially committing treason. Naval blockade starts to be established of rebel-held areas.

1775-1776: ***Invasion of Canada.*** Sep 1775, Benedict Arnold leads a force through the wilderness. British abandon Montreal. Arnold besieges Quebec in winter. Attempts an assault but this is beaten off with Arnold wounded, his colleague killed, and nearly 400 captured. Reinforcements arrive. May 1776, rebels blunder into major British positions at (b) Trois Rivières. British push invaders back towards Ticonderoga.

1775-1776: ***Water wars.*** 1775, revolutionaries capture small sloops giving them control of Lake Champlain and the N-S wilderness route towards Montreal. 1776 both sides work on rushed building programme. (B) Lake Champlain. Americans under Benedict Arnold use shoreline and wind to hold off a superior British force, then escape in the night. But the stragglers are overcome and the British control the waterway. Success is too late to facilitate British attack on Ticonderoga, but British superiority is secured for the duration of the war and facilitates raids and supply lines. 1780, HMS Ontario disappears in a storm over on the Great Lakes.

1776: ***Declaration of Independence.*** Jan, Thomas Paine publishes Common Sense, arguing for an independent republic. June, resolution introduced to Congress declaring independence. A drafting group is formed. July, notwithstanding some opposition Congress votes 12:0 on the final text (New York abstains).

1776+: ***Commerce raiding escalates.*** Numerous small-scale engagements by the small Continental fleet and by large numbers of privateers, causing significant damage to British trade. Many of these vessels themselves end up blockaded and destroyed.

1776: ***Attempt on Charleston.*** Jun 1776, British move on South Carolina thwarted at (b) Sullivan's Island. A hastily-constructed fort protecting the city repels the expeditionary fleet.

1776: ***Boston to New York.*** March, British troops withdrawn from Boston which is no longer tenable, and shipped to Halifax. Washington takes the city, then moves forces to New York. July-Aug, British fleet arrives. Significant local Loyalist support. (B) Long Island. Washington mauled, but critically manages to flee at night across the river. Staten Island Peace Conference. Futile negotiations, possibly however contributing to the preservation of Washington's forces. (B) Harlem Heights. Failed attempt to ambush British results in large skirmish. (B) White Plains. Retreating Washington further obliged to withdraw. (B) Fort Washington. Remaining Continental garrison subjected to assault; nearly 3000 prisoners.

1776-1777: ***Washington counterattacks.*** Dec 1776, (b) Trenton. Washington crosses the Delaware (at the prow of a rowing boat) to lead a surprise night time attack on a garrison at Christmas. Jan 1777, (b) Princeton. Cornwallis advances on Trenton and Washington intercepts. Mixed results on the field; Washington fails to secure gains, but British equally forced out of most of New Jersey. Continental Army survives the first winter despite terms of service running out.

1776-1777: ***A road through the wilderness.*** 1776 after Canada success, Burgoyne halts campaign recognising winter difficulties and aims to take Ticonderoga in the coming year, and to push down to cut off New England's link with the other colonies. That fort's defences are meanwhile prepared in anticipation. July 1777, Burgoyne's forces arrive and spot key flaw in defensive positions. Fort abandoned. (B) Hubbardton. Rearguard surprised by swifter-than-expected British vanguard. But Howe reverses the original decision for his forces to link up with Burgoyne. Burgoyne sends a column into Vermont for supplies, which is destroyed by a far larger force at (b) Bennington. Aug, (b) Oriskany. Diversionary siege of Fort Stanwix triggers battle between Patriot and Loyalist units, with

Mohawks on both sides. Loyalist victory but fort holds out and prevents reinforcing of Burgoyne. Sep, (b) Freeman's Farm. Heavy fighting results in withdrawal of Benedict Arnold and the Patriot forces, but also large British casualties which they cannot afford. Burgoyne decides against pushing immediately on, but doesn't retreat as he is expecting to link up with British units advancing inland from New York under Clinton. He is becoming outnumbered 3:1. Oct, (b) Saratoga. British testing force repulsed, Burgoyne falls back but fails to seize last chance to retreat still expecting reinforcements. He is cut off by a force now six or seven times larger than his own and forced to capitulate.

1777: ***Howe's alternative thrust.*** Having left Burgoyne to his own devices, Howe lands forces in Pennsylvania intending to seize the population centre of Philadelphia, which has a strong Loyalist presence. Sep, (B) Brandywine Creek. A strong defensive position is turned by a British flanking movement. Washington is defeated but not destroyed as Howe pauses to consolidate. (B) Paoli. Named after a tavern. British launch a night time bayonet assault with their light infantry on a patriot encampment. The militia swiftly rout and scatter. Howe captures Philadelphia. Oct, (b) Germantown. Washington fails in an attempt to surprise Howe's army. His larger force breaks up and is routed, but again not destroyed. However, notwithstanding the successes against Burgoyne, Washington's own forces are now badly demoralised and facing a grim winter with little logistical support.

1777-1778: ***Winter in Valley Forge.*** Washington somehow keeps the Continental Army in existence despite lack of supplies, and shortages of key essentials. Conway Cabal: Washington is almost relieved of his command after dissent in the army becomes known. Prussian officer Steuben trains the troops. Howe meanwhile is replaced by Clinton, who is ordered to evacuate Philadelphia owing to the threat of a French fleet and base himself at New York. Washington advances to intercept the army on the march.

1778+: ***Foreign intervention and the point of no return.*** 1777 French covert aid begins. Arrival of Lafayette aged 19, appointed a Maj-Gen without pay. 1778 after Saratoga, to pre-empt possible reconciliation between London and rebels negotiating from a position of strength, France recognises American independence and signs formal Treaty of Alliance. March 1778, Parliamentary Peace Commission. Parliament offers Congress all demands except independence: rejected by Congress. Sep, Benjamin Franklin appointed diplomatic representative to France. 1779, Spain declares war on Britain. Hardliner John Adams appointed as peace negotiator by Congress. 1780, colonial forces move into West Florida and capture Mobile. 1781, capture Pensacola and secure West Florida. Dutch and Britain at war.

1778: ***New grand plans***. Howe is replaced by Clinton, who is ordered in context of the imminent French threat to evacuate Philadelphia and base himself at New York. Washington advances to intercept the army on the march. Jun, (b) Monmouth. The Continental attack is poorly managed and only rescued by the arrival of the main force under Washington himself. British withdrawal is able to continue, though this in itself confirms strategic failure and the threat from the French. 1778 new push in the south, British capture Savannah and Augusta in Georgia. 1779, failed siege of Savannah by joint Continental-French force.

1778-1779: ***John Paul Jones.*** 1778, failed attempt on the major coaling port of Whitehaven. Failed attempt to kidnap the Earl of Selkirk from his house. 1779 on Bonhomme Richard raids northeast England. (B) Flamborough Head. A confused scrap and an American victory.

1779: ***Penobscot Bay Fiasco.*** British expedition lands in northern Massachusetts. Large rebel force sent to dislodge them from Fort George (a conceptual rather than physical set of defences). Arrival of a British force triggers panic and rout, leading to the utter destruction or capture of the large rebel fleet.

1779: ***Controversy and a key port***. 1778, French fleet under Comte d'Estaing arrives off Rhode Island. British destroy their own ships in Newport to prevent capture. But French failure to act in concert proves disastrous: a drop in army morale, desertions and the lifting of the longstanding Continental siege follow. This in turn leads to a sally by the now-reinforced defenders and (b) Rhode Island confirming the withdrawal. D'Estaing also declines an attempt to attack a smaller British fleet, and sails back to Boston. Boston and Charleston riot when they find out, so D'Estaing sails off to the West Indies. Nevertheless, Newport is shortly afterwards abandoned by the British. A large French force lands there and is then penned in by blockade.

1776-1780: ***Espionage.*** 1776, Nathan Hale disguises himself as a Dutch schoolmaster to spy on British positions at New York. After a week's work he is captured and hanged: "I only regret that I have but one life to lose for my country." *A questionable case.* May 1779, a demoralised Benedict Arnold offers to surrender West Point ('The American Gibraltar' – it controls the Hudson and thus can split off New England) in return for money. May 1780, Arnold warns of French troop landings imminent in the north east, resulting in Clinton leaving for there. Sep, Major John André landed near West Point to liaise with Arnold, but his ship is then spotted and has to withdraw. André is forced to return to British lines by land. He puts on a civilian overcoat and has a pass from Arnold, but is captured near British lines by three Americans concealing their identity. Plans of West Point are discovered but realising what has happened Arnold himself flees in time. Washington arrives at West Point rather coincidentally on the day it was going to be surrendered. Oct, Major André hanged as a spy, provoking outrage and creating a martyr.

1779: ***French arrive.*** A large force lands near Savannah but is badly repulsed. 1780, Lafayette personally encourages the French Court to send a larger force, with Washington as the supreme commander.

1780-1781: ***Brief wobbles.*** Supply crisis as Continental currency increasingly considered to be worthless. May 1780, two regiments mutiny at Washington's camp owing to serious lack of pay and food. Suppressed by threat of force, leaders hanged. Jan 1781 mutiny amongst soldiers in New Jersey, suppressed by same means. As things stand, British forces still occupy Canada, much of the south, and key ports, while French bankruptcy looms.

1780-1781: ***Action in the Carolinas.*** Jan, Clinton lands in South Carolina and captures Charleston – a major victory as the entire southern army surrenders with it and the revolutionary navy is destroyed for a generation. Cornwallis is given local command. May, (b) Camden. Col Banastre Tarleton drives off militia units and mauls the Continental regiments that stand. South Carolina secured in British hands, but reliant on foraging for supplies thus reducing local support. October, (b) King's Mountain. American versus American battle. Loyalist force smashed and captured by Revolutionary force, followed by war crimes. Local Loyalists deterred. Jan 1781, (b) Cowpens. Rash and anticipated attack by Tarleton is repulsed, leading to the surrender of most of the British force. Another small engagement that had a disproportionate psychological impact. Apr, (b) Hobkirk's Hill. Continental move on Loyalist garrisons thwarted. Smaller British force routs Continentals attempting to enfilade, but British outposts looking exposed. Sep 1781, (b) Eutaw Springs. Continental army pushed back, rallies then takes the British camp and starts looting while British secure a key strongpoint. British forces pull back to Charleston.

1781: ***Articles of Confederation (drafted 1777) ratified:*** a central Continental government officially called into being.

1781: ***Virginia decides***. Cornwallis pushes into Virginia. March, (b) Guilford Courthouse. Though outnumbered over 2:1, he assaults enemy positions and drives the rebels from the field. Despite capturing Norfolk the plan to conquer the Carolinas is halted and shifted to Virginia. Richmond evacuated and burned; several revolutionary leaders including Jefferson very narrowly escape ("Jouett's Ride"). (B) Green Spring. Lafayette is lured into attacking what he thinks is a smaller force. His men narrowly escape, but rather than pursue Cornwallis pushes on to Yorktown. Cornwallis (like Burgoyne before him) is expecting reinforcements from New York so does not withdraw when Continental and French forces concentrate. Washington feints on New York but shifts from his original plan and marches south and joins Lafayette instead. Cornwallis is now besieged by a superior force. With the fleet split while the French concentrate, the Royal Navy temporarily loses control of local waters to French warships at (b) The Capes/Chesapeake. This prevents evacuation, reinforcement or resupply for Cornwallis over a critical few weeks, while French reinforcements can ship through. Major Cochrane slips through on a rowing boat and successfully delivers despatches to the besieged. A plan to sneak the army away by boat is defeated by a sudden squall. Oct, Cornwallis surrenders. The relieving British force arrives five days too late. A quarter of the British army in North America is captured, but at the time even this is not considered conclusive.

1781-1783: *The road to peace.* 1781, expanded Continental peace mission formed. Feb 1782, Parliament votes to halt offensives, thus allowing military resources to be deployed elsewhere. Mar, fall of Government of Lord North. Rockingham Government enters peace talks. Meanwhile fighting continues globally with the European powers. Hudson's Bay raided by the French. April 1782, (b) The Saintes: Royal Navy triumphant in the Caribbean. Feb 1783, British declare a halt to hostilities. Sep, Treaty of Paris signed. Independence of the United States is recognised along certain borders; US fishing rights confirmed in British North America; debts to be paid by individuals; Congress to urge that confiscated estates be restored; release of prisoners; no prosecutions for supporting a side; free navigation of the Mississippi; withdrawal of British troops, with captured static artillery to be left behind; captured official and private papers to be returned; any military gains made after the signing of the treaty (and before news of it arrives) to be ignored and evacuated as well. Britain to retain Canada but as it stood in 1763 not 1774, thus the hinterland would become part of the US. Peace of Paris. Amongst global territorial changes, Spain to retain captured West Florida, gain East Florida, both of which had remained loyal; it also assumes the claim on Louisiana. The terms cause the British Government to fall.

Low Season 1783-1815

The new republic reorganises itself, whereas the surviving colonies are forced to adapt to changed circumstances. The hinterland is unlocked, and a last attempt by the Americans to reunify their continent by force is repulsed, creating a Canadian national identity in the process.

Period Events

March 1783: *Military putsch averted.* Washington steps in as the Continental Army is restless at the bankrupt government's failure to pay them off. Troops discharged in Nov, Dec Washington resigns.

1783: *Loyalist exodus.* Several thousand leave New York alone; perhaps 100,000 in total will have emigrated. New towns set up in Canada. 1784, New Brunswick separated as a new colony to ease administration.

1783: *Ex-slave exodus.* British refuse point blank to hand over escaped slaves, including those who served in the Black Pioneers or supporting the Royal Artillery, considering it "an act of justice due to them from us". Instead a register (Book of Negroes) is created as the basis for possible compensation (never paid). They emigrate largely to and via Halifax, though further assistance is limited. 1791, one of their number, Thomas Peters, lobbies for inclusion in the Sierra Leone colony plans. 1792 a group establishes the settlement at Freetown.

1783-1784: *The Long Winter.* Extreme weather conditions (also prevalent in Europe) tentatively being linked with an Icelandic volcano, Laki, whose eruption has utterly devastated the island.

1785-1795: *Brake on settlement lifted.* 1785, first plots. Northwest Indian war begins. 1787, Northwest Ordinance establishes rules for forming new states in newly-settled lands. 1791, Fort Recovery Massacre: US suffers greatest military defeat against Indians with three quarters of a force of 1200 killed. 1795 Treaty of Greenville ends Northwest Indian war and secures region for US. New states created as settlers push out – in addition to the thirteen original colonies accepting statehood by 1790, there is Vermont (from New York, 1791); Kentucky (from Virginia, 1792); Tennessee (1796); Ohio (1803); Louisiana (1812).

1786: *Shays' Rebellion.* Farmers in Massachusetts seek debt relief, which does not come. Daniel Shays amongst the leaders of armed gangs that obstruct courts sitting on debt cases, and lift prisoners. Suppressed by force.

1787: *Constitutional Convention.* Machinery of the American state agreed. Federalists and Anti-Federalists begin their campaigns on the level of centralisation the new state should ultimately have, what should be considered implicit, and the level of democratic rights permitted. Constitution ratified as federalists win, but the concept of a Bill of Rights and more democratically established lower house is conceded. 1789 twelve amendments proposed, ten accepted in 1791 as the Bill of Rights.

1788: *A New America.* Botany Bay colony in Australia founded.

1789-1790: *Nootka Sound.* 1789, Spanish seize British ships in the far north west. Crisis escalates, Spain backs down. 1790, Nootka Sound Convention: both countries to have equal rights, temporary residencies.

1789-1791 *Establishment of federal government.* Washington the first President. 1790, agreement to move the capital to a specially constructed site. 1791, Washington rejects Hamilton's proposal for a national bank.

1775-1792: *Pounds and Pence.* 1775, "Continental" paper notes printed. 1781, first national bank set up for the central government. 1785, Dollar introduced as a common currency. 1791, first central bank. 1792, Coinage Act regulates coins.

1791: *Constitutional Act.* Quebec becomes Lower Canada. Settled Canadian hinterland becomes Upper Canada. Each to have a legislative assembly, an appointed executive, and a governor. French civil law is preserved in Lower Canada.

1793+: ***Construction of the National Capital (I).*** 1793, laying of the Capitol cornerstone. 1795, foundation collapses, and funding also slips. North and South wings (only) completed in time for 1812 war.

1793+: ***Construction of the National Capital (II).*** 1793, York (Toronto) founded as a fort and associated settlement. Capital of Upper Canada shifted there from Newark (Niagara-on-the-Lake) owing to threat of US involvement now Britain and France are at war; intended as a stop-gap move. 1796 capital confirmed: population of 400 plus 200 soldiers. 1796-1798 brick parliament buildings built. 1807 church built.

1783-1794: ***Continuing US-French links.*** 1784 visit by Lafayette. 1789 French revolution: Lafayette supports moderate revolutionaries and is appointed commander of the National Guard. 1791 his position deteriorates after the royal family attempts to flee the country and is caught, and then by the Champs de Mars Shootings (a larger version of the Boston Massacre). He ends up a counter-revolutionary prisoner but is ultimately released. American links with France are frayed by the extreme revolutionary events of 1792-1794.

1791-1794: ***Whiskey Rebellion.*** Southern and western distillers run a tax revolt using lessons learned from Boston. Support extends to those suffering economic hardship. Troops despatched by federal government but conciliatory stance follows from the Federalist party.

1759+: ***Interior explored by British.*** Wilderness is mapped out. James Cook. 1759, charts the St Lawrence during the invasion of Quebec. 1763-1767 detailed mapping of Newfoundland. 1778 during Third Voyage explores the north west coast. Voyages of Samuel Hearne. **1769-1772,** Hearne explores the Hudson Bay hinterland, on huge hikes carrying the barest of necessities. He reaches the far northern sea by foot. Philip Turnor. 1778-1789 surveys routes in the hinterland. Alexander Mackenzie. 1789, follows the river named after him to the Arctic. 1792-1793 completes first westward crossing of North America, narrowly missing on the Pacific Coast encountering George Vancouver who over 1792-1794 is mapping the region. David Thompson. 1792, starts surveying for the Hudson's Bay Company. 1797, controversially quits to join its competitor the North West Company. Tasked to conduct an emergency survey of the 49th Parallel in the wake of Jay's Treaty to identify exactly where company posts are sited. 1798-1801 further surveying trips. In response to Lewis and Clark expedition from US, 1806-1809 and 1811 explores Columbia region. Simon Fraser. 1808, explores the Fraser River. Ultimately secures British title to the west of the Rockies above the 49th Parallel.

1793-1800: ***US International involvements.*** 1793, US support for French combating slave revolution in Haiti leads to numbers of French exiles in America. Proclamation of Neutrality in the war involving Revolutionary France. 1794, Citizen Genêt Affair. French ambassador attempts to use US ports to support French privateers. 1795, Jay Treaty; resolves certain remaining issues from the Treaty of Paris; compensation of British creditors, British forts that are still on US territory. Border between the Lakes and the Rockies set at the 49th Parallel. Pinckney Treaty; commercial access rights and frontier agreed with Spain. 1796, Washington's Farewell Address recommends small armed forces, no additional foreign alliances, and avoiding European wars. French start seizing shipping. 1798, Alien and Sedition Acts designed to limit threats arising from expats agitating from exile in America. Kentucky and Virginia Resolutions: two Jeffersonian states overrule these Acts which have aspects that suppress free speech. XYZ Affair. Americans take umbrage at being expected to bribe French diplomats. US-French treaty abrogated. 1798-1800, The Quasi-War. Undeclared large scale naval war between USA and France.

1801-1805: ***First Barbary War.*** On independence, American vessels are no longer under Royal Navy protection. Agreement reached with Morocco but Algiers prefers piracy. 1793 becomes an issue when Algiers-Portugal peace treaty exposes Atlantic. 1795, tribute terms negotiated for safe passage. 1801, Algiers demands better deal. Corsairs go to war. 1803 war spreads to involve all Barbary states. USS Philadelphia grounded, crew captured, vessel later burned by US raiding party. 1804 more ships sent, Tripoli blockaded. Mercenary group cobbled together seizes a town in support of a claimant to the throne. Peace deal buys back US prisoners, but piracy subsequently resumes.

1803: ***Louisiana Purchase.*** 800,000 square miles for $15 million. Size of the United States doubles. 1804 Lewis and Clark expedition departs to explore the region. Nov, Treaty of St Louis: questionably legal deal cedes 50 million acres of Indian land rights.

1806: ***Burr Conspiracy.*** 1801, tie over Presidential elections – Jefferson elected, Aaron Burr defeated and thus becomes Vice President (rules subsequently changed). 1804, Burr's career ruined after he kills Hamilton in a duel. 1806, claim that Burr involved in a conspiracy to freelance carve off Spanish colonies. Burr is initially acquitted then leaves the country in a hurry.

1807: ***Abolition of the Slave Trade Act.*** British slave trade outlawed. But the Royal Navy has limited resources and legal rights to police the trade in vessels flying other flags.

1806-1812: ***Foreign tensions.*** France and Britain obstruct neutral US shipping trading with the other. 1807, HMS Leopard engages USS Chesapeake as the latter refuses to allow a boarding to identify deserters. President Jefferson pushes an embargo effectively stopping foreign trade. This is economically damaging, hugely unpopular, and is replaced in 1809 with the Non-Intercourse Act embargoing just Britain and France. 1810 Act expires: trade permitted if countries lift restrictions on US shipping – France does, Britain does not. 1811 (HMS) Little Belt Affair: US and Royal Navy ships clash.

1810-1814: ***US intentions on Florida.*** 1800 Spain cedes an ill-defined portion of West Florida to France. This claim accompanies Louisiana on its sale to the USA. 1810, small coastal slice near New Orleans declares independence as the brief Republic of West Florida. US annexes despite initial opposition. Patriot's War. 1812 secessionists briefly seize Ferdinanda and claim US control over Florida. Rebel activity and transgressions trigger attacks from Seminole Indians, escalating into a full blown Seminole war. 1813-1814 two further small slices of West Florida are annexed by the USA but otherwise the attempt is defeated.

1811: ***Tecumseh.*** 1805, Tecumseh's brother has visions and becomes a Shawnee prophet. Build up of an Indian confederacy. 1811, (B) Tippecanoe. Pre-emptive American expedition marching on the Indian capital Prophetstown triggers an Indian attack, which is eventually repulsed. Prophetstown settlement burned and temporarily dispersed. But Confederacy incentivised to ally with British.

1811: ***Great Midwest Earthquake.*** Gigantic tremors centred on New Madrid. Mississippi starts flowing upstream in places. Catastrophe averted by the simple absence of major population centres.

1811: ***Red River Colony.*** Lord Selkirk granted huge concession west of Lake Superior for settlement. A slice dips south of the 49th Parallel.

1812: ***Start of Mr Madison's War.*** March: war nearly breaks out with France over loss of US shipping. News of British climb down (characteristically) arrives too late. Anticipating an easy conquest of Canada, President Madison unleashes the War of 1812 in June. Opposition swiftly grows, in turn provoking pro-war rioting in Baltimore. July, Hull's army invades Upper Canada then retreats to Detroit. British general Brock and Tecumseh force the larger American force to surrender. Brief cease fire.

1812: ***Attempt to cross Niagara.*** Nov 1812, (b) Queenston Heights. American column attempting to cross the river is smashed, but Brock killed. (B) Frenchman's Creek. Americans take a key defensive position but invasion force falls apart.

1812-1813: ***Northwest campaign.*** Indiana Territory fighting between Indians and US garrisons. Sep 1812 General Harrison arrives to begin offensives against Indians. Jan 1813, (b) River Raisin/Frenchtown. American force attempting to retake Detroit badly defeated, a number of prisoners killed by Indian allies.

1813: ***Niagara Front reopened.*** Apr 1813, American forces land off York. Attack on Fort York leads to it being abandoned. Magazine blown up and by freak of layout causes heavy casualties amongst advancing American forces, who consider it a deliberate act.

Americans briefly occupy York, wreck a number of buildings and burn its legislative assembly, turning the locals completely against them. British naval reinforcements denied to the Great Lakes flotilla. (B) Fort George. Americans occupy a foothold east of the Niagara.

1813: ***Battle for the Great Lakes decides the North West.*** Sep 1813, (b) Lake Erie. British risk battle against stronger force to open supply lines. Decisive US victory secures them control of the lake, allowing capture of Amherstburg and Detroit and cutting off Tecumseh. Canada unlocked. Oct 1813, (b) of the Thames. Retreating half-starved British and Indians engaged by Harrison. Frontal attack routs the regulars. Tecumseh killed. Indian confederation falls apart, ending British hopes of a separate state for them. North West in American hands. Naval fighting and a ship building race continues though, and skirmishes occur across a wide and largely isolated front. 1814, British regain supremacy in Lake Ontario. May 1814, successful British raid on key supply point of Fort Oswego.

1813: ***Niagara Front stabilises.*** June 1813, (b) Stoney Creek. Outnumbered 5:1, a British force exploits excellent intelligence to launch a night attack. Large losses but both American generals captured, leading to US withdrawal via a depot ruined by a British raid to their rear. (B) Beaver Dams. Laura Secord acts as the Canadian Paul Revere, allowing British to intercept American advance with Indians. Many US prisoners, Fort George garrison disinclined to push forward. US front contracts. Dec 1813, Burning of Newark. Original US orders provided for shelter of the locals to be left, but none provided despite it being midwinter. Considered a further US atrocity, triggering British raid and burning of Black Rock and Buffalo. British capture Fort Niagara. May 1814, Americans raid and burn Port Dover.

1813: ***St Lawrence secured.*** Feb 1813 British garrison of Prescott turns a drill on the frozen river into a dash to storm Ogdensburg. The town is taken, the Canadian womenfolk loot the houses, and after withdrawing the US garrison is not restored, meaning the threat to the supply route is ended. Jul-Aug 1813, Murray's Raid on US settlements along Lake Champlain. US joint offensive. Plan to push one army up the Champlain and another down the St Lawrence, converging on Montreal. Oct 1813, (b) Chateauguay. De Salaberry's outnumbered French Canadian militia defeat an American army south of Montreal. Nov 1813, (b) Crysler's Farm. An outnumbered force of Anglo-Canadians defeats the second US thrust.

1813-1814: ***East Coastal campaign.*** Apr 1813, successful British raids on Chesapeake Bay while blockade in place. June, (b) Craney Island. American fort repels move on Norfolk. Boatload of volunteer French ex-prisoners of war fighting with the British massacred; in return Hampton is subsequently sacked. Jul, successful raid on Ocracoke.

Raiding continues into 1814.

1813-1814: ***Creek War.*** Creek civil war brings in American intervention from Mississippi Territory. This escalates after Fort Mims Massacre. Mar 1814, (b) Horseshoe Bend. Andrew Jackson storms hostile Creek positions. Some losers flee to Spanish Florida. Creek allies and enemy alike forced to cede territory to the US at the Treaty of Fort Jackson.

1814: ***Second attempt on the Saint Lawrence.*** Mar 1814, (b) Lacolle Mills. Move on advanced British position draws in reinforcements and is repulsed.

1814: ***Brown's Campaign.*** Jul 1814, Gen Brown takes Fort Erie. (B) Chippawa. British pushed back after a misjudged advance. (B) Lundy's Lane. Americans outflank the British and seize key guns. Counterattacks fail. Fighting is bloody. The Americans withdraw and the invasion is halted. Fort Erie is later evacuated after a costly failed attempt to besiege it.

1814: ***Burning of the Capital.*** 1814, defeat of Napoleon frees up British reinforcements. Aug 1814, British troops land in Maryland. (B) Bladensburg. Larger American blocking force utterly routed. Washington occupied. The President's dinner is eaten in the President's house. Government though not private buildings are burned, patent office spared. Naval force raids Alexandria up the Potomac. Sep 1814, (b) North Point. British defeat blocking force as they advance towards Baltimore, but lose General Ross. Royal Naval bombardment of Fort McHenry fails, and the star-spangled banner still waves. Attack on Baltimore is halted. Proposal to move the capital from its wrecked site back to Philadelphia is defeated.

1814: ***Advance into Maine.*** British land advance shudders falteringly into US territory. Sep 1814, naval force under Sherbrooke captures Castine.

1814: ***Failed invasion of New York.*** Sep 1814, Prévost leads British advance via Lake Champlain, reminiscent of Burgoyne's old plan. (B) Plattsburgh. Naval squadron acting in support is defeated, so with supply route cut off the army withdraws.

1814: ***Gulf Campaign.*** British attempt to support Creek results in General Jackson seizing Spanish Pensacola, Nov 1814. Dec 1814, (b) Lake Borgne. US flotilla overcome trying to halt British landings in Louisiana. (B) Villeré. Fight in plantations outside New Orleans. Jackson withdraws but British halt. Jan 1815, (b) New Orleans. Confused British attack on strong US defences. Many British casualties, including Pakenham and his deputy. British withdraw. Feb 1815, the force captures Fort Bowyer in annexed West Florida.

1812-1815: ***Frigate-on-Frigate actions.*** Jul 1812, HMS Shannon captures USS Nautilus. Aug 1812, USS Constitution captures HMS Guerrière. Oct 1812, USS United States captures HMS Macedonian. Dec 1812, HMS Java scuttled after engagement with USS Constitution. June 1813, HMS Shannon boards and captures USS Chesapeake. Mar 1814, HMS Phoebe captures USS Essex off Chile. Jan 1815, USS President captured trying to run blockade.

1814-1815: ***Hartford Convention.*** Dec 1814, secret meeting of New England Federalists who oppose trade laws and the war. Reports of this emerging just as the war is ending prove fatally damaging for the Federalist movement.

Dec 1814: ***Treaty of Ghent.*** Ceasefire between the two countries and with the Indians, whom Britain shall not arm. No loss of territory, with disputes to be settled by commission. Both countries (article 10) to use their best efforts to utterly abolish slavery, which is "irreconcilable with the principles of humanity and justice". The last attempt to unify North America under a single government ends.

Appendix 2
A Word Before You Leave

To a refined English observer, the American Revolution is the world's greatest tragedy to date. Put aside for a moment the advantages the French will make of it, and the inspiration proffered to godless revolutionaries in future years. Consider simply how history would have turned out if a settlement had been reached, and the Atlantic remained united. What might have been achieved by the Empire with such an additional hinterland of genius and drive? What loss to British politics, the cession of so many vigorous minds? For the inhabitants of the new nation it has provided a massive boost of course, though at some considerable financial and human cost. Yet we cannot but fear for what will come of the innate divisions between such differing states confined under a common, and parochial, political roof.

The Revolution is not, however, total. Of Britain's 26 North American colonies, she keeps half. That includes claims on the land mass of half the continent, even if it is the frostier, undeveloped part with the polar bears. Brave Canada will no doubt still have a critical contribution to play in its own right on the imperial and world stage.

For now though the War of 1812, and the persistent threat of the Royal Navy, convinces American politicians there will be a cost attached to further military conflict with its neighbour to the north. British financial investment provides crucial opportunities to develop the expanding republic. Language links as well as ongoing levels of immigration maintain and develop cultural ties. London for its part meanwhile is strongly aware of the ballooning resources and power of the growing state. The result is a peculiar development in world politics; a largely undefended and truly massive border, and the settlement of disputes - which do continue - by peaceful means. The Convention of 1818 will, mostly, demilitarise the Great Lakes, and push the border line out west to the Rocky Mountains along the 49th Parallel. There'll still be scares and occasional tension, but common sense and the incentive for peace will prevail.

This means that in the future, your chances of joining your regiment to take in the sights of a (smouldering) East Coast will be much reduced. New York stays top of your itinerary in all seasons, but for a different style of gentlemen's clubbing. So pack your top hat, a walking stick and a picnic box. Forget the bombardments: a more tranquil and satisfactory holiday exploring the delights of North America is to be had instead.

Appendix 3
Acknowledgements and Further Study

The nature of the landscape, cultures and history of North America inspired a large body of striking paintings over the Georgian and Victorian eras. Many can be found in local and national museums, especially of course in London and in North America itself.

This book was inspired by a series of anniversaries. The first was the 250th of the signing of the Treaty of Paris (10th February 1763), which received precisely zero recognition in the UK. The second was the bicentenary of the War of 1812, and the realisation in turn that just fifty years after the high water mark of British North America, that anniversary was then being celebrated by the blockading of the Chesapeake by the Royal Navy and by raids into modern day Ontario and New York State.

The author's academic focus in postgraduate days was directed towards French Canada. English language analysis understandably has tended to zoom in on the fight for Québec and the story of Wolfe. French speakers of course have access to a separate and distinct community of historians. A fascinating and strangely jingoistic insight can be gained by reviewing the material produced a hundred years ago by chanoine (later abbé) Lionel Groulx.

A similar bias applies to a number of other histories that exist from even closer to the period. One example is the otherwise free-flowing History of the Rise, Progress and Termination of the American Revolution by Mercy Otis Warren (1805). Yet - understandably - there is a dearth of Loyalist literature covering

their melancholy story as reviewed from exile. A consequence of this was long to allow the 'Patriots' a broadly unchallenged interpretation of events in North American print. If this, equally but more openly biased, publication helps to remind readers that there were two sides to the complex disputes, it has served a key purpose.

We highly recommend a visit to the Smithsonian Museums in Washington DC, and their online journal provides a feast of material. The JSTOR website contains an admirable number of academic articles providing the answers to a wide range of technical questions any investigator might ponder. Colonial Williamsburg offers a location that's miles ahead of being a mere theme park, but also runs a well-presented and informative website (one example is on etiquette, where it carries a 110 point guide by the young George Washington). The Parliamentary Archives also contain a small variety of original and unexpected source material, such as the records on military punishments cited.

07955 007206

About the Author

Dr Lee Rotherham is an historian with two postgraduate degrees on Québec. His survival skills were honed by idly wandering around Montréal on the hunt for second hand book stores during its worst winter on record. An army reservist, it's thus appropriate that from his dealings with the Canadian Armed Forces he is a Member of the Order of Good Cheer/L'Ordre du Bon Temps. This is a Nova Scotia fraternity, originally set up by Samuel de Champlain, which commemorates the terrible winters of the first colonists and the social environment that got them through it. With beer, his accent betrays an alarming French Canadian twang.

His background proved useful when he was taken on by rebel MPs in Parliament, who were fighting against the development of a federal European state and wondering what was coming out of Brussels (at that time the most interesting documents were, strangely, only being released in French). He has since counselled a number of front benchers, leading to a role as the adviser to a delegate at the Convention on the Future of Europe. Since its federalist President compared it to the founding Convention of the United States, Lee in turn was happy to oblige by supporting the minority of delegates fighting for states' rights instead.

In addition to getting squirrel-bedecked woodland pulped to cover the EU, public sector spending, and waste, he is also the author of The Discerning Barbarian's Guidebook to Roman Britain, together with a history of Britain's national debt from Boadicea to David Cameron, and a wee tome on the Scots.

Playing the 'what if...' game, he would have been a Loyalist in the mid-1770s, a Federalist in the 1780s, and a Jeffersonian after the Peace of 1815. But he would have posed for a portrait beside the White House before burning it down.